*Radnorshire:*
*A Historical Guide*

# Radnorshire:
# A Historical Guide

by

*Donald Gregory*

First published in 1994
Revised edition: 2009

© Text Donald Gregory

ISBN: 978-1-84524-141-4

Cover design: Sian Parri
Maps: Ken Gruffydd

First published in 1994 by Gwasg Carreg Gwalch

Revised edition published in 2009 by Llygad Gwalch,
Ysgubor Plas, Llwyndyrys, Pwllheli, Gwynedd LL53 6NG
℡ 01758 750432 🖷 01758 750438
📧 books@carreg-gwalch.com
Web site: www.carreg-gwalch.com

The undermentioned are the owners of the copyright of the
following illustrations and have kindly permitted their use:
The Radnorshire Wildlife Trust for the two photographs of Gilfach
The Llandrindod Festival Committee for the Victorian street scene.

**BY THE SAME AUTHOR:**
Wales Before 1066 – A Guide
Wales Before 1536 – A Guide
Wales After 1536 – A Guide
Country Churchyards in Wales
Yesterday in Village Church and Churchyard (Gomer Press)

*The author gratefully acknowledges his indebtedness to all that*
*W. H. Howse wrote about Radnorshire and to the Radnorshire Society,*
*whose Transactions have proved invaluable;*
*to Helen, who took most of the black and white photographs*

# Contents

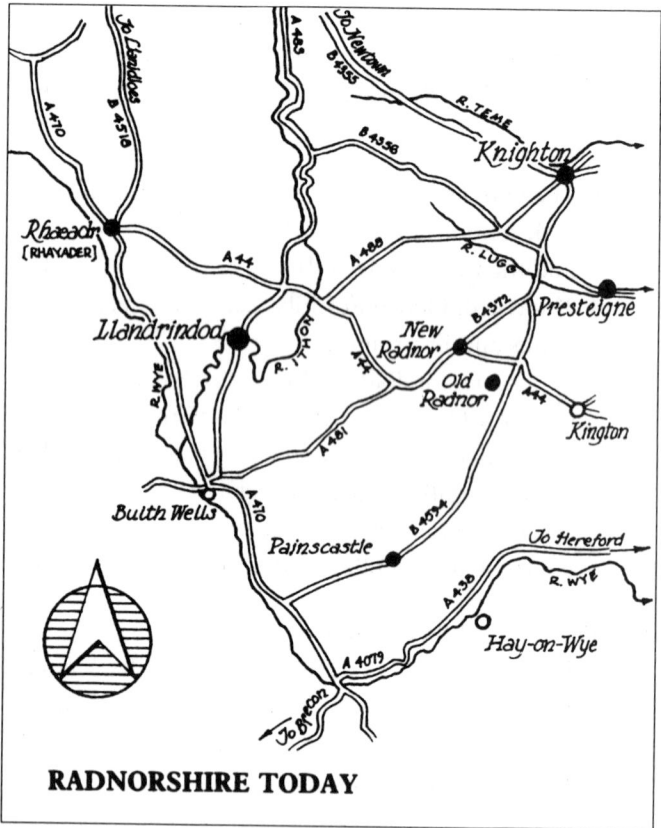

**RADNORSHIRE TODAY**

# Foreword

I have an interest to declare; I am biased in favour of Radnorshire (in Welsh, *Maesyfed*), to which my family removed in the early 1920s, when my father became Postmaster of Llandrindod. We were strangers from the London area but we received nothing but kindness from the people of Llandrindod, who took us in and made us welcome members of the local community. According to G. M. Trevelyan, the man who has no bias to control, rides a sorry nag safely to market; perhaps readers may make excuses for me if occasionally I seem to gallop!

I spent five happy teenage years in Radnorshire, years that left vivid memories, some of which have been retained into old age, like finding a dipper's nest under Shaky Bridge at Cefnllys (today's structure may be made of concrete but it still keeps its name!), like skating in the moonlight on the Lake, or tobogganing down the Brifty or watching our next door neighbour, the Reverend Jonathan Evans setting out for church on Sunday mornings, sporting a shining top hat.

Occasionally, I accompanied my father, when in the course of his work he visited country districts, where he either checked the accounts of the local post offices or walked with the rural postmen in their long treks over the hills. Here I first became familiar with Radnorshire's remote countryside of moors and hills, here I grew to identify birds and flowers, which until then I had only known about from studying cigarette-cards, which were the main source of such information to town boys in the 1920s. I trust that the credulity of readers will not be overstretched when I assure them that on one of these journeys, after visiting Bleddfa, my father stopped to buy a gallon of petrol (for our three-wheeler Morgan) and a dozen eggs, and paid eleven pence (old money!) for each commodity. Now I live in the neighbouring county of Shropshire, from where for more than twenty years I have been privileged to pay innumerable visits to Radnorshire, whose treasures I have greatly enjoyed introducing to chosen friends.

To those familiar with this part of Wales, Radnorshire still exists as a separate and distinctive entity, despite the provisions of an act of Parliament, which in 1974 saw fit to lump together Radnorshire, Brecknockshire and Montgomeryshire into the vast administrative area of Powys, comprising one quarter of the whole of Wales. Brecknockshire, which really belongs to south Wales, and Montgomeryshire, which looks to the north, likewise see themselves as separate and distinctive entities. Radnorshire alone sits in the middle of Wales, wild and remote in parts, underpopulated and wholly delightful to those who like to see around them so much evidence of the past surviving into the present. The past seems to linger longer here.

Radnorshire, which became an English-style county by the Act of Union in 1536, when the earlier division into Elfael in the south and Maelienydd in the north came to an end, is mostly bounded in the west by the river Wye, which rises on Plynlimon (*Pumlumon*), and in the north-east by the Teme, which further on in Shropshire joins the Severn. The county has four main centres of population, Llandrindod, Knighton, Rhayader and Presteigne; they are all fortunate enough to be situated on rivers, the Ithon at Llandrindod and Teme at Knighton, the Wye at Rhayader and the Lugg at Presteigne.

# List of Maps

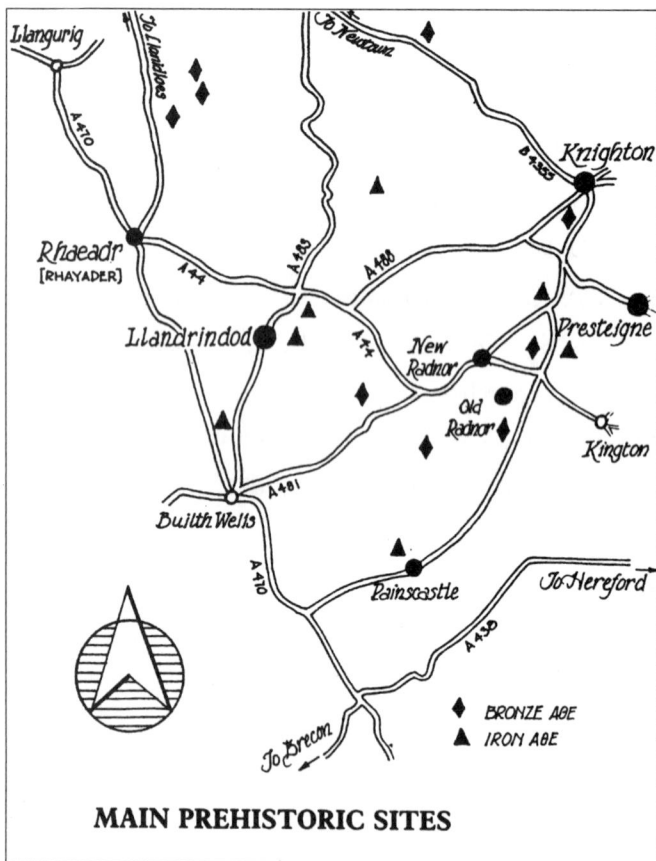

Llangurig

To Llanidloes

To Newtown

Knighton

B 4355

Rhaeadr
[RHAYADER]

A 470

A 44

A 483

A 488

Llandrindod

A 44

Presteigne

New
Radnor

Old
Radnor

Kington

Builth Wells

A 481

A 470

Painscastle

To Hereford

A 470

A 470

To Brecon

◆ BRONZE AGE
▲ IRON AGE

**MAIN PREHISTORIC SITES**

# I. Before 1066

## a. In prehistoric times

Radnorshire was probably the last part of Wales to be settled in prehistoric times, their first inhabitants finding it possible to eke out an existence in the Teme valley, south-east of the Radnor Forest around Old Radnor, in the upland areas further south around Glascwm and further north around Rhayader. This settling-in will have taken place more than four thousand years ago, the arrival of these first inhabitants coinciding with a providential change in the climate about 2000 BC, which made settlement more feasible in the warmer, drier conditions. These prehistoric newcomers tend to be associated with the transitional culture covering the end of the New Stone Age and the beginning of the Bronze Age; these pioneers were primarily farmers, who cleared the land of trees in order to plant their crops and graze their sheep and cattle.

The name of Beaker Folk is often given to them, because in many of their burial places, the so-called round barrows, squat drinking vessels have been found. Round barrows are the earliest prehistoric field monuments to be found in Radnorshire, although few of them have yet been fully or properly investigated. Sometimes a round barrow held the ashes of but one cremated body; rarely do they contain evidence of more than two or three burials. Of the rituals which accompanied the burials nothing at all is known.

Before describing the sites of some of these Bronze Age barrows something should first be said about the evidence of other Bronze Age activity in the county, especially in the Old Radnor district, where standing

13

stones may still be found in situ. The best-known of these puzzling groups of stones is known as the Four Stones (GR 245608), which are situated near a minor road which links the hamlet of Kinnerton to the A44; here four glacial boulders were set up in a circle, with the flat surfaces facing the middle. Just why Bronze Age man erected this monument no-one knows; there are other standing stones in the neighbourhood, one only a quarter of a mile east of the Four Stones, and another pair of stones may be seen not far away in a field near Kinnerton church. There is little doubt that this was an area of Bronze Age settlement, as close to the Four Stones in a farmyard on the A44 stands an unexcavated round barrow.

The area immediately north, north-east and east of the Four Stones is archaeologically important because apart from the various standing stones already mentioned (and there are others too thereabouts) at GR 252613 near Rough Close Farm in 1966 sixteen flints were gathered from a collapsed round barrow, subsequent investigation in the adjoining field bringing to light no fewer than another seven hundred flints, along with potsherds and fragments of cremated bones. In addition, only a mile away to the south is Old Radnor, whose very large parish church, the biggest in the county, was built on the top of Bronze Age earthworks, which are still very obvious to the passer-by.

There is also clear archaeological evidence of a certain amount of Bronze Age occupation a few miles further west. Halfway along the A481, which runs in a N.E. direction from Llanelwedd (site of the 1993 National Eisteddfod) to the Forest Inn, near Llanfihangel Nant Melan, is the ancient hamlet of Hundred House, immediately south of which on both sides of the river Edw will be found the sites of round barrows, now grassgrown (Bryn Llwyd 113543). Shortly after leaving Hundred House a track will be seen on the right hand side of the main road which leads to a large round barrow, Giants Grave, GR 141544, situated about halfway between the A481 and the historic village of Glascwm. Between two and three miles further along the A481, at a point only about half a mile short of the Forest Inn, a track leads south-east to what is labelled MOUND on the Ordnance Survey map, where four standing stones point to a (presumably) unexcavated round barrow, GR 157569. Back on the A481 on the other side of the road, almost opposite the path to the Mound will be found half a mile to the north-west Graig Fawr round barrow, GR 144579. To complete this outline survey of Bronze Age activity in the district another site should be mentioned, that of a standing stone, GR 142588, which is a mile west of the Norman motte and bailey, Castell Crugerydd, GR 158592, lying just off the A44 between the Forest Inn and Llandegley.

Moving north to Knighton (*Trefyclawdd*, the town of the dyke) to look for Bronze Age tumuli in the Teme valley, it should first be recorded that in the 1930s a round barrow was discovered half a mile west of Knighton, when the road to Llandrindod was being widened. The first indication of such an unexpected discovery was the unearthing of a burial urn, which was turned up – and damaged – in the initial digging of the road. The site is now known as the Jackets Well barrow because of its proximity to a well of that name, which in much earlier times had been called Edward's Well, whose consecrated waters had been much sought after by those looking for cures for sprains. Readers who would like to find out more about this archaeologically happy piece of road-widening are advised to consult the Transactions of the

Radnorshire Society for an authoritative account. North-west of Knighton in the Teme valley, between Knucklas and Beguildy, three Bronze Age tumuli survive; their Grid References are 228767, 222771 and 209783, this last site, which is in a field next to the river and is maintained by the owners of Bryndaenog, being well worth a visit.

Finally, in the search for Bronze Age evidence the Rhayader area has to be looked at; this part of the survey is strictly for enthusiasts only, because, although there was quite probably more Bronze Age activity here than elsewhere in the county, surviving evidence on the ground is becoming increasingly hard to find, despite the clear marking of sites on Ordnance Survey maps. Three and a half miles south of the town, but just west of the river Wye and therefore just inside the former county of Brecknockshire, is the village of Llanwrthwl, in whose churchyard is a standing stone, six feet high, which almost touches the south wall of the church, GR 975637. As the church is on a round, raised site, the likelihood is that men in the Bronze Age buried their dead there in a round barrow and then erected the tall stone as a grave marker. Many, many centuries later, in the sixth century, A. D. Gwyrthwl, a Christian missionary who is credited with having built the first church on that site, probably chose that place because it had already acquired an aura of sanctity as the burial place of his prehistoric predecessors. This stone at Llanwrthwl, like several other similar ones in Welsh churchyards, is believed to date from the Bronze Age; it is interesting to note that in the same neighbourhood a gold Bronze Age amulet was dug up, which is now in the safe custody of the museum of Brecon.

Other Bronze Age sites around Rhayader include a standing stone (Maen Serth); two former tumuli, just west of the A44, one mile east of the town; a tumulus, labelled on the map Bancgelli, GR 980708, west of the B4518, which runs north from Rhayader to St Harmon; and a mile and a half further on, again west of the B4518, another tumulus is marked, GR 983723. North of St Harmon, where the Victorian diarist Kilvert had his first living, there is a group of three round barrows, up a farm road, east of the B4518, GRs 990740, 9900739 and 992741. Another site thereabouts is the Mount, GR 012755, situated between two streams, two miles north-west of Bwlch y Sarnau on the minor road to Pant-y-dŵr. Three miles north of Pant-y-dŵr, readers who refuse to take No for an answer will be further rewarded by the sight of a round barrow and several standing stones, GR 964775 and GR 954773.

About two and a half thousand years ago mankind was on the march again in western Europe; as a result new immigrants from the mainland of Europe arrived in the British Isles, where many of them soon crossed the Severn and the Wye, shortly after 500 BC. These new arrivals were the ancestors of the Welsh, who spoke a Celtic language, which in the course of time developed into modern Welsh. Some of these first Welshmen made their homes in Radnorshire; of the four Celtic tribes believed to have colonised Wales around this time, the Silures, who mostly settled in the south of the country and the Ordovices, who were concentrated in the north, probably contributed most to the influx into Radnorshire. These people are said to have introduced the Iron Age; the label will suffice, provided it be remembered that for many years they probably still depended on bronze tools and weapons; when, however, sources of iron ore were gradually discovered in Britain, these Celts soon developed the necessary techniques for extracting the ore and putting it to use in the manufacture of agricultural tools and military weapons. These Iron Age Celts were aggressive, warlike people, who succeeded in imposing their will on the local inhabitants, before presumably intermarrying with those who survived the initial onslaught.

Visual signs in Radnorshire of this long Iron Age occupation are not as obvious as are those of the Bronze Age predecessors; this is because the latter buried their dead in round barrows, whereas their successors in the Iron Age seem not to have paid any attention to the ceremonial burying of their dead, thus depriving modern archaeologists of the chance to excavate their grave goods. What may still be seen, however, are the signs of the way in which they fortified their settlements, within the security of which they lived and grew their crops. In the early years of the settling-in process such fortifying was probably necessary in order to protect themselves and their crops against other equally aggressive Celtic settlers, as well as against wild animals. The defensive attitudes learned at that time became a source of strength to them, when in after years, in the first years of the Christian era, the Romans occupied southern Britain before casting covetous glances at settlements on higher land far to the west.

Of the Iron Age fortified camps, whose descriptions now follow, those chosen provide the imaginative observer with some idea of their purpose and their importance. Starting in the area around Old Radnor, where much evidence of Bronze Age activity has already been shown, two Iron Age sites impress: the first, known as Castle Ring, (GR 266636) lis N.N.E. of Evenjobb, between that village and Beggar's Bush, just west of Offa's Dyke. It stands about a thousand feet above sea level and occupies a circular site with a double rampart which encloses about two acres; it has two entrances. The second fort which is at Burfa (GR 284610) is very much larger, containing about twenty acres, and seems to have had secondary as well as primary defences. Unfortunately, in recent years the whole area has been so thickly forested that it is not possible for the layman to sort out the complexities of Burfa Camp.

Ten miles south-west of Old Radnor is the village of Painscastle, the approach to which from Old Radnor is along ever narrowing green lanes; today's village amounts to little more than a cross-roads, a triangular green, an inn, a Nonconformist chapel, a forge, a handful of houses, and, up a lane behind a farm in the very middle of the village, a high green mound. Much will be written later in this book about the long and continuous history of Painscastle (GR 168463), but comment here will be restricted to the bare mention of the fact that on this high green mound the history of Painscastle began, when men and women of the Iron Age came and settled there, defending themselves with sturdy ramparts.

Continuing this survey of Iron Age sites in a clockwise fashion, the next stop will be made at Llanelwedd, where above the Royal Welsh Showground looms to the north-east the rocky ridge of the Carneddau, on whose heights will be found signs of three Iron Age habitations. First, Gaer Fawr (GR 058531), the strongest and the largest of the three encampments, has impressive ramparts, which enclose about two and a half acres. Next, quite close to Gaer Fawr, on a nearby craggy site, is Caer Einion (GR 063531), which, being better protected by nature, needed only two ramparts. The third site, Cwmberwyn Camp (GR 073548), is some distance further north-east of the Carneddau, not far to the west of the hamlet of

Llansantffraed-in-Elvel; it is protected by only one rampart. All three sites are best visited together on the same day in order to understand and appreciate their importance.

Less than three miles north of Cwmberwyn two more Iron Age sites await enthusiasts, if they are on foot; if, however, they depend on cars, they will first have to drive to Llandrindod. Take the steep and narrow road to the south of Llandrindod, which passes the south side of the lake, before climbing up past Old Llandrindod church and the club-house of the golf course, before descending into a delightful, almost uninhabited valley where the road ends at Carreg Wiber farm. Above this isolated farmhouse a promontory fort looms, its name the same as that of the farm, Carreg Wiber Bank (GR 084595). The name means dragon or serpent stone and refers to an ancient stone, which once stood at the side of the road near the farm (GR 081594). This area around Carreg Wiber is thought to have been much occupied previously in the Bronze Age, a theory to which several finds of Bronze Age axes in the locality (the most recent in 1972) bear witness.

The second site in this area is quite near Carreg Wiber but hardly accessible from it, even on foot. Better to return to Llandrindod and again drive south of the town, getting from the Broadway into Cefnllys Lane, which after a mile and a half ends at the river Ithon at Cefnllys (GR 089615), a delectable spot, where there is a woodland trail, a picnic site, and a bridge over the river, known as the Shaky Bridge. This latter is a concrete structure which replaced the wooden bridge of former times, where, as mentioned in the Foreword, the author, in his boyhood, found under its wooden timbers the nest of a dipper.

This wonderful stretch of the river from the Shaky to

the Alpine bridges, which flows round the steep-sided flanks of Cefnllys Hill, is in truth a historical palimpsest; a much longer visit will be paid to Cefnllys, when medieval Radnorshire is under consideration, because, in the Middle Ages, a planned town grew up there between the river and the hill, under the watchful patronage of the Mortimer family, who held sway from their castle on Cefnllys Hill. History started here when, in the Iron Age, early men erected their huts on the hill and proceeded to protect them with such sturdy ramparts that, centuries later, when new settlers came upon the scene, they incorporated these ramparts into their own defensive system.

The last visit to Iron Age sites necessitates a short car journey north of Llandrindod on the A483; four miles north of Crossgates and one mile north of Llanddewi Ystradenni may be seen, just to the east of the main road, two peaks, both of which are crowned with Iron Age forts. The more westerly one, which seems to have no name (GR 114698), though quite small had several lines of defence, whereas its near neighbour to the east, Cwm Cefn-y-gaer (GR 121699), though much larger, has but one rampart, but that one stoutly built of stone.

## b. Under Roman occupation

The very uncertainty of life for people in the Iron Age, suggested by their fortified encampments, must have been very considerably increased when tales of new settlers in the valleys eventually reached their ears. It was about the year 60 AD that Roman troops were for a short time stationed on a low hill above the river Wye near Clyro (GR 227435); little can today be seen on the ground, though aerial photography confirms the existence there of a formerly fortified site. About ten years later Roman soldiers were probably first seen by Celtic tribesmen, who had ventured forth from their protected homes on the Carneddau ridge or from Carreg Wiber above the Ithon. It is very likely, however, that the Roman impact on Radnorshire was minimal, although it is known that a Celtic leader, Caractacus, made his last stand against the invaders thereabouts. Our only certain knowledge of the Romans in those parts came from the fact that they built, just north of Llandrindod, a fort, known as Castell Collen (GR 055628), a road built by the Romans north-eastwards from Carmarthen through Llandovery enabling them to secure their lines of communication.

By 75 AD Wales had become as Roman as it was ever to be, their administrative headquarters being at Chester and Caerleon. These two key places were linked by roads that passed through border lands, where clearly the Romans needed a number of forts. Such a fort was set up at Castell Collen, which, like the rest of those wayside strong points, was manned by auxiliary troops, who, though thought to conform to Roman standards of efficiency, were regarded as inferior to members of the legions, who anyway received more money for their services. Castell Collen was built to house at most a thousand men, less if cavalry were to be stationed there. The original fort, set up probably in the middle 70s, covered about five acres and consisted of wooden buildings, surrounded by a ditch and an earthen rampart. By the beginning of the third century the Roman military position had changed; conquest had been achieved but containment of the Celtic tribesmen was still thought necessary. At Castell Collen the fortified area was halved, as was the garrison, but stouter buildings of stone replaced the more flimsy wooden ones. The long life of the Castell Collen fort probably underlines the reluctance on the part of the Celts to tolerate the Roman occupation of their homeland. In the west wall of the church porch at Llanbadarn Fawr, two miles NE of Llandrindod, a stone has been set, which probably came from Castell Collen, two miles away. It bears the inscription VAL FLAVINI.

While in residence in Castell Collen, the Romans over the years built practice camps, where troops performed their drill, refined their tactics and generally speaking treated the area in much the same way that the British army in later years treated Salisbury Plain! Of the eighteen such practice camps, which were chronicled as being located on Llandrindod Common, south of the town and about two miles from Castell Collen, traces of fourteen of them survive, though the evidence is more convincing when seen from an aeroplane than when searched for on the ground, though even on the ground several are still identifiable at GR 054602. There is also, at GR 054590, vestigial proof of what is thought to have been another Roman fort, Caer Du. In addition to the practice camps, the Romans also set up a great many so-called marching camps, which were temporary camps, often for one night only, when troops were on the move; one can but have retrospective sympathy with soldiers, who, at the end of a long day's march, had to set to and provide safe accommodation for the night!

The Roman occupation of Britain, which began in 43 AD, officially came to an end in 410, but thirty years previously the last Roman soldier left Wales, enabling the men and women of the Iron Age to return in relative safety to their homes in the hills, their way of life only marginally affected by the departing army of occupation. It may come as something of a surprise to some readers to learn that Christianity, which had officially been outlawed in the Roman Empire (bear in mind that it was the Romans who had crucified Christ), first came to Wales in the uniforms of the Roman army. In about the middle of the third century AD two Roman soldiers, situated in Caerleon, were put to death for the crime of being Christians. In the following century, in 314, the Emperor Constantine himself was converted to Christianity, which thereafter became one of the leading religions of the Roman Empire. There is, however, no record either of Christianity being practised by the Roman auxiliaries, stationed in Castell Collen, or of the Christian religion surviving anywhere in Wales after the departure of Roman soldiers.

## c. The spread of Christianity

The flimsy social fabric of Britain collapsed at the beginning of the fifth century, as the support of the strong arm of Rome was withdrawn; chaos prevailed and the Britons reverted to paganism. Geographical Wales, however, was largely spared this putting back of the clock, because contacts by sea with men across the channel were maintained and even increased at this time; along these all-important trade routes, before long Christianity came back to the western Celts, thanks mostly to the evangelising efforts of missionaries from Brittany, of whom Illtud was pre-eminent. As a consequence throughout the fifth and sixth centuries Christian settlements were set up in Wales, long, long before the Pope dispatched his envoy Augustine to take back Christianity to eastern Britain at the very end of the sixth century.

These early missionaries have for centuries been referred to as saints, but in fact the appellation is purely an honorary one, except in the case of St David, who had been officially canonised by the authorities in Rome. Four of these numerous sixth century missionaries have distinct associations with Radnorshire. They were all contemporaries of St David, who is credited by tradition, unconfirmed by any proof, of having himself come to Radnorshire and built a religious cell at Glascwm, about which more will be said later. These four itinerant men of God in Radnorshire were Teilo, Padarn, Cynllo and Cewydd (Teilo and Padarn had already accompanied St David on pilgrimage to Rome and Jerusalem); when each man moved into Radnorshire, he will have chosen a suitable site (in all cases near a supply of fresh water), and there erected a wooden cross. Nearby he will have built a wooden hut to live in and then made the site safe by throwing up a bank of earth, unless, as often happened the missionary chose to build inside an existing enclosure. This religious settlement was known as a llan, a place enclosed for religious purposes. Whether these early llans were put up as simple monastic places of retreat or as potential focal points of missionary activity, there is now no way of knowing. In some parts of Wales the latter reason may well have prevailed but in wild, remote and sparsely populated Radnorshire, the intention uppermost in the founder's mind was probably to find and make safe a suitable place for private religious contemplation.

Before citing the areas in the county where these early missionaries set up their llans, some mention has also to be made of other early Christian communities with whom there are no known associations with missionaries but whose ancient ambience is attested to by visual evidence that survives. Three Christian sites within ten miles of each other a few miles south of Knighton all

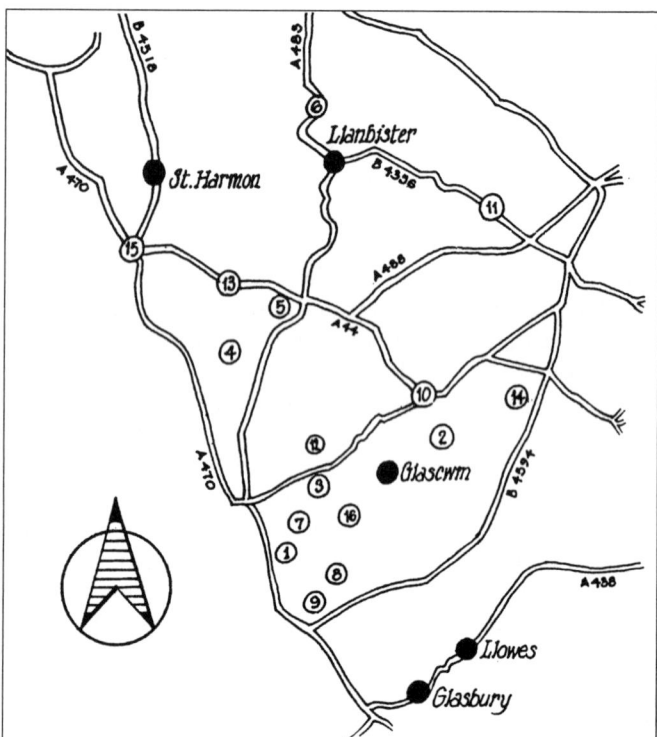

LLANNAU O

1 *Aberedw*
2 *Colva*
3 *Cregrina*
4 *Disserth*
5 *Llanbadarn Fawr*
6 *Llanbadarn Fynydd*
7 *Llanbadarn-y-Garreg*
8 *Llanddewi Fach*

CLASAU ●

9 *Llandeilo Graban*
10 *Llanfihangel Nant Melan*
11 *Llangunllo*
12 *Llansanffraid in Elfael*
13 *Nantmel*
14 *Old Radnor*
15 *Rhaeadr/Rhayader*
16 *Rhulen*

# SITES OF CLASAU AND EARLY LLANNAU

suggest early Christian llans. Old Radnor church (GR 250591), though dating mostly only from the fifteenth century thanks to the exigencies of war in the early years of that century, yet stands in a round churchyard amid Bronze Age earthworks; even within this post-medieval church there is too a font, which, according to expert opinion, cannot belong to any century later than the eighth. Five miles to the west along the A44 lies the village of Llanfihangel Nant Melan (GR 180582), whose church, rebuilt in the nineteenth century in imitation of Herefordshire's Kilpeck, breasts a pre-Christian site; the churchyard is round, and within it is a ring of extremely ancient yew trees. The same evidence of a pre-Christian site can be seen a few miles further west at Llansantffraed-in-Elvel (GR 100548). The fact that again and again in Wales it can be seen that early Christians chose, whenever possible, to build on sites already made sacred by religious forebears many centuries previously, encourages the belief that there may well have been early Christian settlements in these three churchyards.

Of the four Radnorshire missionaries Teilo was the best-known in Wales generally, although Cynllo seems to have been the busiest and the most influential locally. Teilo, at times a close colleague of David himself, is believed to have built his first llan at Llandeilo in Carmarthenshire, where he probably spent most of his life and where he died; he did at least once move into Radnorshire, when he chose a site in the Wye valley, where west of Painscastle, he established a llan at Llandeilo Graban (GR 094447). The hilly country just north of the place is still known as Llandeilo Hill, on the southern slopes of which the Ordnance map marks a historic site, curiously named St Teilo's Barn. Today's church was probably built in the fourteenth century and was certainly renovated in the late nineteenth century, but it is in the middle of a round churchyard, the banking of which adds weight to the theory that Teilo himself thus protected his original llan.

Padarn, whose name was sometimes latinised into Paternus, is rightly famous for the monastery he established at Llanbadarn Fawr (which today is a part of Aberystwyth), but there are also three llans in Radnorshire, dedicated to him, which he is credited with having set up in the sixth century, one, also called Llanbadarn Fawr (GR 088643), two miles north-east of Llandrindod, another on high ground north of Llanbister, Llanbadarn Fynydd (GR 098778), and the third in remote country above the Wye valley, east of Aberedw, Llanbadarn-y-garreg (GR 113487). The first of these churches today, almost completely rebuilt in late Victorian times, except for the porch, which is still adorned with a marvellous medieval tympanum, once gave shelter for a while in the twelfth century to Giraldus Cambrensis, when that unfortunate cleric was besieged by the people of the parish, after the archdeacon had fallen foul of them! Llanbadarn Fynydd is remarkable for having today no north side to its churchyard, as the church now stands on the very edge of a cliff above the river Ithon into which, it is to be presumed, the rest of the churchyard once fell. Llanbadarn-y-garreg remains a plain and unadorned, white-washed old church, beside the river Edw, far from the ways of men and with an ambience all its own.

Third of the early holy men of Radnorshire was Cewydd, who, as far as is known, looked for a secluded spot wherein to build and to retreat in religious and social isolation. Accordingly he set up a llan in a field near the river Ithon at Disserth (GR 034583). Here in this deserted place (hence its name) Cewydd chose to live his solitary life of contemplation; a few miles away in the Wye valley below Builth near the spot where the Edw flows into the Wye, the church of Aberedw (GR 080474) bears Cewydd's dedication, though proof is lacking that the hermit of Disserth was personally responsible for the formation of the first llan there. Today's splendid churches at Disserth (mostly thirteenth century) and at Aberedw (fourteenth-fifteenth centuries) and their historically important churchyards will be referred to again, much later, in this book.

Last to be mentioned of these pioneers but by no means the least in importance is Cynllo, who had four churches dedicated to him in the north of the county, at Rhayader, Nantmel, Llanbister and Llangunllo. Of the early llan at Rhayader (GR 969682) nothing survives; all is Victorian save for an early medieval font, and even Cynllo's dedication has now gone, replaced by that of Clement. Five miles south-east of Rhayader, well above the A44, is the church of Nantmel (GR 034663), which enjoys a hilly situation in a very large circular churchyard, while the present church at Llanbister (GR 111734), situated just off the busy A483 road from Crossgates to Newtown, is but the latest in a succession of churches built on that round, steep and extremely hilly site. Towards the end of the twelfth century Giraldus Cambrensis spent a night or two in the church, when he was looking for recruits for the Third Crusade, and there six hundred years earlier Cynllo had set up his llan, near a well, which up to the middle of the twentieth century continued to supply the needs of the local community. About six miles east of Llanbister is Llangunllo (GR 212713), whose llan was also established by Cynllo rather later in the sixth century, by which time Llanbister, having become a clas, acted as a mother church to a number of dependent llans, like Llangunllo.

Many scholars believe that Radnorshire at this time was so very remote and off the beaten track that its main attraction to these wandering men of religion was the wide choice it afforded of suitable places of retreat. Nevertheless Christianity rapidly spread after the establishment of these llans, making it essential that further provison should be made for the spiritual welfare and opportunities for worship for these converts. In time, then, as the number of Christian conversions increased, the responsibilities of the llans often tended to change; when llans, which had been primarily set up for meditation, became centres of Christian worship, they sometimes became mother churches, as at Llanbister. Such a mother church often became a clas, a small monastery, under the watchful eye of an abbot, who caused mission churches to be built in the locality. These clasau, from small beginnings, in the course of time, acquired considerable importance because not only did they cater for the spiritual welfare of their converts, both in the mother churches and in the out-stations, but they also became cultural centres, where scholars forgathered and made their learning available to others. In Radnorshire there were at various times five of these spiritual and cultural rallying-points, at Llanbister, St Harmon, Llowes, Glasbury and at Glascwm, those at Llanbister and Glascwm being probably the earliest and most important. The clas at Llanbister, centred on that most imposing of ecclesiastical sites, must have served a very wide area indeed, as there were certainly small churches dependent on the mother church at Llangunllo, Llananno, Llanbadarn Fynydd, Llanddewi Ystradenni and Llanfihangel Rhyd Ithon. In later days another clas was established in north Radnorshire, three and a half miles north-east of Rhayader, at St Harmon (GR 984728), whose church was dedicated to St Garmon, a sixth century holy man, who had other churches dedicated to him, outside Radnorshire, at Capel Garmon, Llanarmon-yn-Iâl, Llanarmon Dyffryn Ceiriog and at Llanfechain. The present church at St Harmon, though almost entirely rebuilt in the early nineteenth century, stands in a round and raised churchyard in an area which is the richest in Radnorshire for evidence of Bronze Age occupation. Today's visitor should note some good eighteenth-century tombstones and should remember that the Victorian diarist Kilvert, who had been a curate in south Radnorshire at Clyro from 1865 to 1870, was vicar of St Harmon from 1876-1877; he noted in his diary that St Harmon 'is the only Welsh-speaking parish in Radnorshire'.

The three other clasau were in the south of the county; the one at Llowes (GR 192418) was established in the middle of the seventh century, when St Meilig came down from Strathclyde; all that now remains of those early days is the round churchyard. Most of the church was rebuilt in Victorian times, although it provides welcome shelter to an eleventh-century cross, which formerly stood in the churchyard. A few miles to the south-west is Glasbury, whose Welsh name, Y Clas-ar-Wy, clearly reveals its early importance, when St Cynidr built there (GR 177392), but alas, his clas was built very close to the river, which at a later date caused the site to be abandoned.

On a number of counts Glascwm, the clas in the valley, is historically one of the most interesting places in Radnorshire; history is still there on the ground for those with eyes to see and imagination to interpret. The village (GR 157532), which is situated in a beautiful, wooded valley, sheltered by the wild Radnorshire hills, can be reached via the the A481, which has to be left just west of Hundred House. The narrow road thereafter is circuitous, the reward surprising; the first sign of an approaching settlement is furnished by a large house on the righthand side, beyond which very soon appears on the other side of the road a very large church. Further down the road into the main part of the village is the Old Vicarage (read Kilvert for his description of a visit he made there in May 1871, when the house was twice its present size – see Appendix to this chapter), the Post Office, and the Youth Hostel, which was once the village school. Round about are a number of houses, four of which were inns in the nineteenth century, when a drovers' route passed through Glascwm. At that time there was also in the village a racecourse.

To this secluded spot in the sixth century came the first Christian missionary, whom tradition insists was St David himself; if this indeed was so, then Glascwm will have been the furthest north St David took his message. Certainly in the sixth century a llan was created here, the actual site possibly having been dictated by evidence of previous occupation in prehistoric times. Bronze Age men lived hereabouts; mention has already been made of a large round barrow, Giants Grave (GR 141544), which can be reached in a pleasant walk from Glascwm over the hill to Hundred House. The present church, the successor to the first wooden hut, stands on the levelled top of a round mound, which the presence nearby of a semi-circle of ancient yews suggests may once have been another round barrow. Over the years this early llan prospered and became a substantial clas, whose mission churches in the neighbourhood, all, like Glascwm, dedicated to St David, included Cregrina (GR 124521), Rhulen (GR

138499), Colva (GR 199532) and Llanddewi Fach (GR 146456). The church today in Glascwm, which dates mostly from the thirteenth century, is surrounded by an extensive churchyard.

One of these mission churches, Rhulen, which is a mile and a half south of Cregrina, deserves a very special mention; it stands apart for its remoteness, its long history and its simple, peaceful beauty. The church, whose nave and chancel are all one, is white-washed, and set upon a mound, whose periphery is marked by gnarled old trees. Once again there is a strong likelihood that the original llan was established in this place because long years before prehistoric people had lived and died there. Today's church, thought to date from about the thirteenth century, bears no mark of any known architectural style; there is no east window behind the altar, which is set in a shouldered recess, as is the entrance to the church, whose door belongs to the seventeenth century. The approach to the church is up a mile-long and very narrow lane, finger-posted Rhulen; it is suitable only for a small car – and an enthusiastic driver!

## d. Offa's Dyke

Back in the fifth century, not long after the withdrawal of the Romans from Britain, eastern Britain was infiltrated periodically by Germanic tribes from Northern Europe. Jutes, Angles and Saxons. After years of inter-tribal bickering, first the northern Saxons, the Northumbrians and then the middle Saxons, the Mercians became the dominant Saxon power. It was in the eighth century that the men of Mercia took the initiative, bringing them into repeated conflict with the Welsh. First these Saxons built

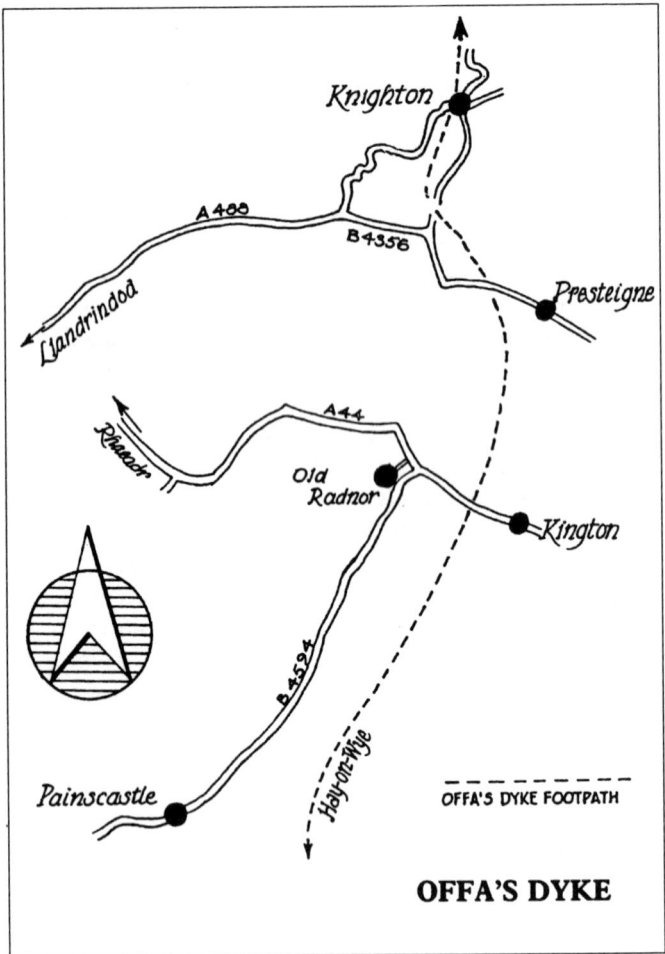

OFFA'S DYKE FOOTPATH

**OFFA'S DYKE**

a defensive line at the northern end of their boundary
with the Welsh (Wat's Dyke), then in the last decade of the
century, probably in about 790, the Mercian king, Offa,
took advantage of one of the rare periods of peace with
his Welsh neighbours to dig the dyke which came to be
associated with his name. This dyke, which was built
further west than Wat's Dyke, ran from the estuary of the
Dee in the north, to the mouth of the Wye in the south.
These great earthworks should not be regarded as a
fortification but rather as a line of demarcation, marking
the boundary between the Welshmen and the Mercians.
That Offa should have felt this onerous task necessary is
a tribute to the steadfast resistance of Welsh leaders, and
more particularly of the rulers of Powys.

At intervals along the dyke significant gaps were left,
whose purpose was to facilitate the passage of men and
goods in both directions. In the early years after the dyke
was finished, a number of mutually agreed regulations
were enforced, one of which made it necessary for a
Welsh guide to meet any party of Saxons who wanted to
move west; among the duties of this guide was to see that
the party returned safely to Mercia and to make certain
that no infringement of the laws had taken place during
the crossing. Likewise, of course, a Mercian guide had
also to escort any Welshmen crossing over into Mercia.
Most of these local rules and regulations, however, dealt
with the inevitable straying of cattle. Radnorshire is
fortunate in that a number of these gaps still survive, of
which the most important is the town of Knighton. In
Radnorshire too, just south of Knighton much of the
original earthworks may still be seen – and walked upon
(its whereabouts will be described in the next section).

As early as in the 1930s enthusiastic walkers, who
knew their history and cared about the past, mooted the

possibility of forming a footpath, which would link up the various surviving sections of the dyke along its whole length. The war interrupted these civilised plans, but with the return of relative sanity in 1945 the passage through Parliament of the National Parks Act gave encouragement and ten years later, in 1955, the Offa's Dyke Path was designated. The goal was finally reached in 1971, when the Long Distance Footpath was officially opened, with its headquarters fittingly set up in Knighton, where most of the pioneering work had been organised under the inspired guidance and leadership of Frank Noble, who taught History in the Town on the Dyke. The path, which runs for a hundred and sixty-eight miles from Prestatyn to Chepstow, is not, nor could it have been, an attempt to re-establish Offa's Dyke itself; it is a new path, which manages to incorporate in it some sixty miles of surviving dyke, much of which is in Radnorshire, whose lucky inhabitants, it is to be hoped, take full advantage of the historic treasure in their midst.

To get a real sense of being on the Dyke Proper take to the Footpath, as it climbs south out of Knighton; three times before it crosses into Herefordshire north-west of Kington, really impressive sections will be traversed, on Hawthorn Hill (GR 288682), east of Beggar's Bush (GR 269640) and south-east of Evenjobb (GR 274628).

*The Four Stones*

Half a mile to the east of them is the Hindwell Pool, with which the Four Stones are associated in folk memory; the Four Stones, into which four local chiefs, according to folk-lore, were turned, and allowed to resume human shape and go down to slake their thirsts in Hindwell Pool, whenever they hear the sound of the bells in Old Radnor church, which is about a mile away. There is a gap between the two stones nearest to the camera which has prompted the thought that there may have originally been a fifth boulder.

*Old Radnor Church and Churchyard*

The prehistoric earthworks, referred to in the text, can be seen in the foreground. Inside the church the ancient font should be studied, as it is thought to be an erratic boulder which, according to ancient local belief, may once have filled the gap in the Four Stones! Certainly the font is much older than anything else in the existing building.

*Maen Serth*

Two miles north-west of Rhayader, high up above the Old Coach Road at GR 944698, is Maen Serth, a standing stone of prehistoric origin, almost certainly belonging to the Bronze Age. A cross, incised on one face, is thought to have been added in the twelfth century AD, to mark the scene of a local murder.

*Church and Churchyard – at Llanfihangel Nant Melan*

To the student of history the churchyard here is even more interesting than the church; it is circular and pre-Christian, probably dating back to the Bronze Age. The yew trees, seen in the illustration, confirm the age of the site.

*Llanbister Church*

This unusually hilly site was first built upon in the 6th century, when Cynllo made it his headquarters; today's church, splendidly restored early this century, mostly dates from the 13th century. The vicar of Llanbister in the first half of the 19th century, the Rev. David Lloyd is one of the three Radnorshire priests' whose colourful lives are described elsewhere in this book.

*St Harmon Church*

This mostly 19th century building is on an ancient Celtic site on which was erected in the 6th century the mother church of a clas. In the raised circular churchyard will be seen pine trees rather than the customary yews.

*Glascwm Church*

St David's church is built on top of a mound, flanked by yew trees, suggesting an earlier pre-Christian occupation of the site.

*Rhulen Church*

Rhulen church is one of Radnorshire's most beautiful and most remote places of worship. Words fail to give an adequate impression of its serene ambience. Bronze Age people probably lived here before Christians set up their llan here in the 6th century.

*Offa's Dyke*

This illustration, which is of Offa's Dyke near Knighton, shows the footpath closely following the line of the dyke.

*Offa's Dyke – Presteigne*

# II.   From 1066-1536

## A.   The enemy at the gate

### a.   The occupation of the Marches

So far readers have been spared the chronicling of warring princes and of political ambitions getting out of hand; elsewhere in Wales the story would have been a very different one, but here in Radnorshire the noise of turmoil was only faintly heard in the far distance. This seemingly idyllic situation was, however, coming to an end when Offa built his mighty earthwork at the end of the eighth century; this suzerainty of the Mercians over the rest of the Saxons, suggested by the leadership of Offa, was to last only for one more generation, since by 830 circumstances had changed for them in two important respects. First the West Saxons of Wessex had succeeded the Mercians as the strongest Saxon power, and secondly a fearsome external threat had developed with the Vikings, making many successful raids and subsequent landings on the east coast of Britain. All the Saxons, faced by this daunting enemy, came together under the leadership of Wessex, whose ruler thereafter became the King of England.

In this ninth century, when the Celts' enemy across Offa's Dyke had become the king of a unified country, Wales too produced an outstanding leader in Rhodri Mawr, who in 844 became ruler of Gwynedd and Powys, adding in the thirty-four years of his reign, much of south Wales too to his domain. In 871, at which time Rhodri was still ruling Wales, Alfred the Great became King of England and successfully assumed the responsibility of containing the Vikings (who in England were known as the Danes). From then until about 950, when another great Welsh ruler died (Hywel Dda), there had been a general understanding between the Welsh and the English, based on their fear of the common enemy, the Vikings. After the middle of this tenth century, however, there was considerable confusion and much anarchy both sides of Offa's Dyke, which was to last for nearly a hundred years, until in fact about 1040, when two strong leaders arose, one Welsh, the other Saxon, men of intelligence, aggressiveness and ambition who were to clash irreconcilably.

When Gruffudd ap Llywelyn, in 1039, became King of Gwynedd, real hopes were raised for a time that Wales might under him become a unified nation; in 1042 the half-Norman Edward the Confessor accepted an invitation to come over from Normandy to become King of England; real power nevertheless remained in the hands of the king-maker, Earl Godwin, the ruler of Saxon Wessex. When Godwin died in 1051, the King appointed Godwin's son, Harold, the Earl of Hereford, to be his right-hand man. The scene was then set for action; for while Harold quickly advanced the Saxon cause, Gruffudd ap Llywelyn, who meanwhile had made himself the first Welshman to rule the whole of his country, seized the chance of acquiring a sturdy ally in the approaching clash with Harold. Gruffudd made an alliance with the old enemy Mercia, whose position too was being threatened by the impending march north from Gwent of Saxon Harold. This unexpected alliance Gruffudd further cemented by marrying the Mercian king's daughter.

In 1061 Harold began his northward advance; he was a skillful organiser and an astute tactician, who always consolidated a new position before progressing further.

Three years later, in 1064, he marched into Radnorshire, where he built himself a castle at New Radnor, before going further north to prepare for the final test of strength with Gruffudd, who was based on Rhuddlan Castle. Poor Gruffudd, harried by the Saxons and deserted by some of his own supporters, was overwhelmed and killed.

The Saxon conquest of Wales now seemed inevitable, especially as Harold became King of England in January 1066, when Edward the Confessor died. Destiny here however took a hand; the dreaded Saxon overlordship of Wales was short-lived as in October 1066 Harold was killed in battle by the invading Normans at Hastings. Wales was soon to be exposed to an infinitely more powerful threat of conquest at the hands of the victorious Normans.

Once he had overcome residual Saxon opposition in England after Hastings, William soon made it clear that he regarded the land beyond Offa's Dyke as his next legitimate area for further expansion. Responsibility for that task he delegated to three of his Norman henchmen, who, from the headquarters they set up along the borders between 1067 and 1071, set about their appointed tasks. These Norman nominees, the newly-created Earls of Chester, Hereford and Shrewsbury, were given virtual carte blanche as Marcher Lords to carry out William's instructions against the Welsh, employing such methods and devising such plans as each saw necessary, without any need for further consultation with government in London. Thus they proceeded to exercise extraordinary authority in what was to prove an unrelenting struggle against the equally determined Welsh.

The Marcher Lords selected strategic positions where they built their wooden castles, which consisted of towers (keeps), erected on the tops of mounds of earth, specifically thrown up for the purpose; these mounds of earth, specifically thrown up for the purpose; these mounds (mottes) were surrounded by wooden palisades beneath which were large enclosed areas, where the soldiers had their living quarters and grew their food. These baileys too were protected by wooden fences and deep ditches, which were often filled with water. In the short term these mottes and baileys were very useful in holding down an area and in providing reasonable security for the garrison, but the strategy was largely a negative and defensive one. The sites of a very large number of these mottes and baileys have survived in the hilly central section of the Marches, especially in the south of Shropshire and in Radnorshire.

As long as Radnorshire people kept their heads down, they were little aware of Norman interference in their lives during the lifetime of William 1st, but after his death in 1087, in the reign of his son, William Rufus, the pace of penetration quickened and in 1095 the castle and lands around New Radnor were given by William II to the scion of another Norman family, Philip de Braose, whose father Robert had fought with the first William at Hastings; before long Philip de Braose became master of most of south Radnorshire as far west as the river Wye. This family, which was, as will be seen, to play such an important part later on in the Norman struggle to impose its will over Radnorshire, hailed from Bruis near Cherbourg; it also received lands in Scotland, where in the course of time its surname changed to Bruce.

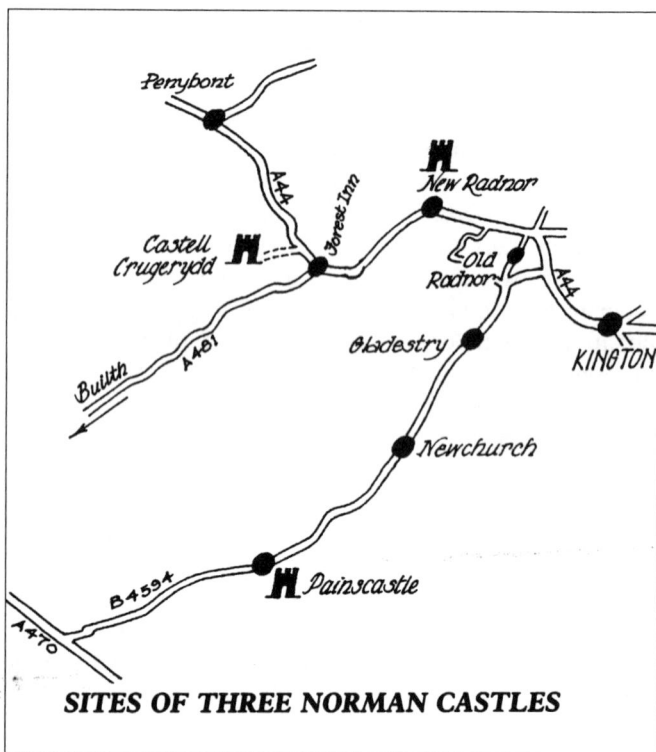

*Penybont*

A44

*Forest Inn*

*Castell Crugerydd*

New Radnor

Old Radnor

A44

A481

*Builth*

*Bleddestry*

KINGTON

*Newchurch*

B4594

*Painscastle*

A470

**SITES OF THREE NORMAN CASTLES**

## b. Norman castles

It is as well, when thinking about castles, at any rate in Radnorshire, to remember that the word 'castle' in origin meant 'a fortified place'; ignore, at least for the time being, pictures in the mind of Windsor or Caerphilly or Caernarfon. In Radnorshire there is surviving evidence, much of it vestigial, of nearly thirty such fortified places of which three have been selected for special attention, those at New Radnor, Painscastle and Cefnllys. All three are reasonably accessible sites, all three are scenically outstanding, and all three have a certain ambience about them, rarely to be found in this fretful age of getting and spending.

To visit the site of New Radnor's castle (GR 211610) today it is advisable to follow the path to the church, the entrance to the castle having been originally nearby. The first castle, a wooden keep, was built by Saxon Harold in 1064 in the course of his march north from Chepstow to confront Gruffudd ap Llywelyn at Rhuddlan; Harold's purpose, apparently, in building a castle where he did was to offset the loss of another castle three miles to the east at Old Radnor, which his Welsh enemy, Gruffudd, had destroyed twelve years previously in 1052. Old Radnor, the most ancient settlement in the district, whose prehistoric origins have already been mentioned, was thus supplanted by New Radnor in the eleventh century, but the adjective 'new' is as inappropriate here as it is in the New Forest! Of the succession of castles, built at various times on this site, under the lee of the south-east corner of the Radnor Forest, nothing can now be seen save the earthworks and the entrenchments; subsequently stone buildings replaced the wooden keeps, excavations in the eighteenth and nineteenth centuries revealing a number of stone arches. New Radnor's castle overlooked the town, which gradually grew up to the east of it to supply the needs of the garrison.

The interest in this area of the Norman emigré family of de Braose began in 1095, when William II (Rufus) gave New Radnor to Philip de Braose, who from his new headquarters in New Radnor castle soon strengthened and expanded Norman authority in the district. For most of the twelfth century the de Braose family's hold on New Radnor was strong, its head in the second half of the century being none other than the infamous William de Braose, who seems richly to have deserved his nick-name of 'The Ogre of Abergavenny'. More will be heard of him when the history of the castle at Painscastle is being described. The Ogre's authority in New Radnor was to be challenged, however, in 1195, when Wales' newly-acquired champion, Rhys ap Gruffudd (The Lord Rhys), marched across from Dinefwr into Radnorshire and captured New Radnor castle in 1196, but this Welsh triumph was short-lived as the Lord Rhys died in 1197; in the following year William de Braose was back again in charge at New Radnor.

The useful life of this strategically situated castle had but one more century to run; in 1209 King John made de Braose give up his castle, although five years later the next de Braose, Reginald, managed to recapture it but in 1216 the King moved against New Radnor and burned the castle to the ground. The ding-dong struggle continued when Reginald returned to New Radnor in 1217, when he reoccupied the site and rebuilt the castle; at his death he left it to his son, another William, who ruled there until 1230, when he clashed with Llywelyn ap Iorwerth (the Great), who had him hanged. This William was the last male de Braose to be master of New Radnor, but his daughter, Maud, who inherited the castle, in 1233 married Roger Mortimer, who proceeded to add New Radnor to the family collection of castles. His grip on New Radnor was for a long time precarious but it seems that he had returned to his possession by 1275, because in that year he rebuilt it in stone. With the death in 1282 of Llywelyn ap Gruffudd removing for a while any Welsh threat to the control of the Marches, the fourteenth century ushered in a much more peaceful era for the Mortimers, who continued to exercise their widespread

The Wye bridge; the old Tollgate; the Red Kite centre;
the north/south, east/west crossroads in the town centre

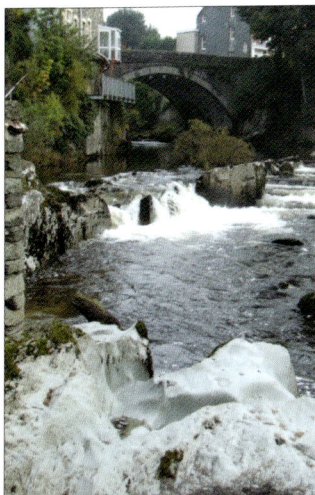

**Gigrin Farm**
**The Red Kite Feeding Centre**
Feeding is at 2pm in Winter & 3pm in Summer
(Birds don't know that we change the clocks!)

**Feeding is at 3 pm**

**Open from**
**1pm - 5pm**

## RADNORSHIRE TOWN: PAINSCASTLE
The Judge's Lodging; the post office; the Lugg river bridge;
the town centre

## RADNORSHIRE TOWN: LLANDRINDOD
A Victorian bandstand; the Radnorshire museum; the lake;
the iron-work character in the town centre

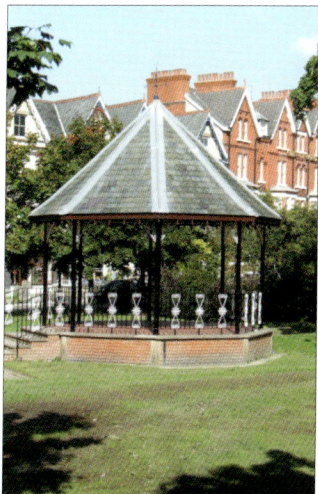

## RADNORSHIRE TOWN: KNIGHTON
The old house; the Offa's Dyke heritage centre;
main street and clock tower

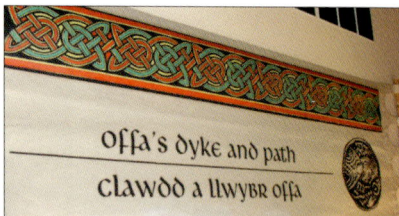

Offa's dyke and path
clawdd a llwybr offa

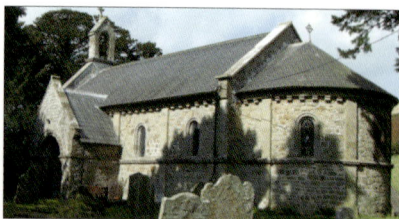

# RADNORSHIRE CHURCHES
## Llanfihangel Rhyd Ithon; Rhulen; Beguildy; Bleddfa

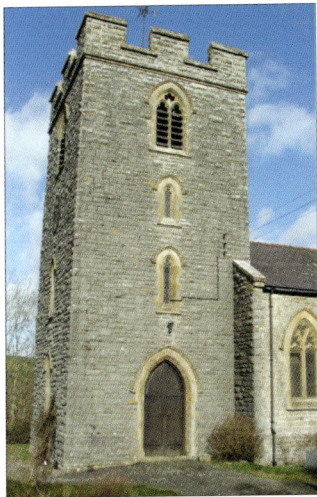

## A RADNORSHIRE BATTLEFIELD
### Bryn Glas, above Pilleth church,
### the site of the historical victory by Owain Glyndŵr's army

## A RADNORSHIRE ABBEY: ABATY CWM HIR
This old Cistercian abbey was sponsered by the Welsh princes
and here lies the remains of the great prince, Llywelyn ap Gruffudd

The ninth-century dyke built as a Wales/England border survives
in many parts of the county – now a long-distance walking path

## RADNORSHIRE RESERVOIRS
### Elan Valley Centre; Cwm Elan; Cronfa Graig Ddu; Cronfa Penygarreg

# A Radnorshire village:
## New Radnor

Tafarn y Ffermwyr (Farmers' Arms) Presteigne; The Hundred House;
Metropole Hotel, Llandrindod; The Radnorshire Arms, Presteigne

## RADNORSHIRE INNS AND TAVERNS:

Radnorshire Arms, New Radnor; Red Lion, Llanfihangel Nant Melan;
Crown Inn, Rhayader; Triangle Inn, Rhayader

**RADNORSHIRE INNS AND TAVERNS:**
The Cornhill, Rhayader; The New Inn, Newbridge-on-Wye;
The Radnorshire Arms, Beguildy; Rhydspence Inn

authority thereabouts, not least from their stronghold in New Radnor.

After a century of non-interference from the outside world, the castle briefly and very dramatically found itself on the stage of history once again at the very beginning of the fifteenth century when Wales' mighty hero, Owain Glyndŵr, passed that way. Twenty years later, by which time Owain Glyndŵr's revolt had long been frustrated, what remained of New Radnor officially passed from the Mortimer family into the custody of the Crown. More than a century later, in 1535, Bishop Roland Lee, President of the Court of the Council of Wales, was sent on an official mission by Henry VIII's right-hand man, Thomas Cromwell, to report on the state of the Marches; in his report Bishop Lee expressed the opinion that the castle of New Radnor was beyond repair but thought that its gate-house might usefully be converted into a prison, for which, in his opinion, there was a great need thereabouts, so prevalent was crime. And so a prison it became, with one of its early inmates being, according to the local record, Lewis ap Morgan, the vicar of Aberedw, whose offence apparently was that he dabbled in 'superstitious practices'.

History's final footnote on the castle was written yet another century later when, in the civil war of the seventeenth century parts of the castle were patched up sufficiently for a royal garrison to hold out for a while until a parliamentary force, which had defeated a royalist detachment in a skirmish at Presteigne, marched westwards and drove the royal garrison out of the castle.

The second castle to be visited is at Painscastle (GR 168463), which involves a very pleasant drive from New Radnor. First take the A44 back eastwards from New Radnor for not more than four miles, when a minor road to the right, clearly labelled Painscastle, leads, after passing through the villages of Gladestry and Newchurch, into a narrow green lane, which eventually opens up to reveal Painscastle. Earlier in this book a passing reference was made to the fact that the history of Painscastle had probably begun on the green mound that rises up in the middle of the village, where people of the Iron Age chose to settle.

In about 1130 a Norman knight, Pain Fitz-John, saw the defensive possibilities afforded by the mound and proceeded to construct a motte and bailey there above the earthworks, left by the earlier settlers. It is just possible that between the time of the Iron Age settlement and the Norman occupation of Painscastle the Romans may have used the site, the thought having been suggested in the nineteenth century by the flimsy evidence provided by hearsay that a Roman mosaic floor had briefly been uncovered in the hillside, when villagers were digging in search of building material. Be that as it may, in the 1130s the mound received a wooden keep, which for a while bore its builder's name, Painscastle. After the death of Pain Fitz-John in 1136 ownership of the castle passed to the same de Braose family, which already ruled from the castle at New Radnor; by the 1190s the succession had gone to William de Braose, who thus for a while was responsible for both places, as well as Abergavenny. It was at this time that he changed its name from Painscastle to Castle Matilda, in honour of his wife. In 1196, however, as has already been seen, the Lord Rhys, the undisputed master of south Wales, captured New Radnor from William de Braose and before long also drove him out of Painscastle, but the death of the victorious Welshman the next year enabled William de Braose almost at once to recapture his castles at New

Radnor and Painscastle, where in 1198 he and his wife had to withstand a very important siege.

By this last decade of the twelfth century an uneasy balance had been reached in the struggle for power in Wales; the Norman Marcher lords had extended their authority deep into Welsh territory, at a time when frequent rifts between the three separate Welsh rulers of Gwynedd, Powys and Deheubarth prevented them from making common cause against the common enemy, the Norman invaders.

The actual siege of Painscastle in 1198 was occasioned by the unbridled and savage cruelty of William de Braose, who had brought about the death in a particularly barbarous fashion of a cousin of the Prince of Powys, Gwenwynwyn, who at once set about to avenge the death of his kinsman. Meanwhile, de Braose who was as shrewd as he was cruel, played successfully on the rivalry existing between the Prince of Powys and the Prince of Deheubarth, persuading the latter to come to his assistance in resisting Gwenwynwyn's attempt to capture Painscastle. A fearsome battle, fatal to the Powys cause, took place in which Gwenwynwyn lost three thousand seven hundred men. William de Braose was in consequence confirmed in his powerful overlordship, while the cause of Welsh unification sustained a serious setback.

This setback to the cause of Welsh freedom, implicit in the failure of Gwenwynwyn to capture Painscastle, was to prove only a temporary one. The bright star of another and far abler Welsh prince was in the ascendant; Llywelyn ap Iorwerth had succeeded to the overlordship of Gwynedd in the 1190s, and by the second decade of the thirteenth century had shown to his fellow countrymen that he was as good a planner and administrator as he was soldier. To such heights had his reputation in Wales risen that, when in 1216 he summoned all the princes of Wales to meet him in Aberdyfi (Aberdovey), they all with one accord acknowledged him to be their leader in the national struggle for independence.

In the very year of this Aberdyfi meeting, however, King John died, and his successor Henry III constituted a much greater threat to the cause of Welsh freedom than his incompetent father had ever done. When Llywelyn, to whom his fellow princes had accorded the unsought title of The Great, stormed into the Marches and captured many a Marcher castle, such as Shrewsbury, Brecon, Hay and New Radnor, Henry III decided to take up the challenge. In the summer of 1231 Henry marched his army out of Hereford and up to Painscastle. Not only did a King of England encamp at Painscastle but he stayed there for the whole of that summer, during which there was much feverish activity as his builders carried out his orders to rebuild the castle more durably in stone, while his civil service was equally well employed, forwarding the affairs of state. For seven weeks in 1231 the whole apparatus of government was transferred from London to Painscastle; records survive that speak of no fewer than one hundred and eighty decrees being promulgated from Painscastle that summer, on matters great and small. It seems quite extraordinary today to the historically-minded visitor, who stands on that lonely and deserted hill, to realise that more than seven and a half centuries previously the King's business had been transacted there, that the King of England had ruled his domain from that windswept hill in remote Radnorshire. His task completed, and Painscastle made strong, Henry III returned to London, thinking no doubt that the ambitious Llywelyn would in future look more carefully before he leaped again. In this expectation he was doomed to be disappointed, when two years later news of Llywelyn's renewed activity caused the King to take charge at Grosmont castle, ten miles north of Monmouth, from which impregnable-seeming eminence he had to endure the humiliating experience of being driven out in the middle of the night by Llywelyn's men, only with the greatest difficulty making good his escape with his Queen in the night attire!

The stone castle that Henry III had built in Painscastle in 1231 required thereafter a considerable garrison; to cater for those needs a considerable community gradually grew up under the hill. This town of Painscastle prospered, despite the damage done by an unsuccessful raid by the Welsh on the castle in 1265. For nearly a century and a half after that time of tribulation Painscastle seems to have enjoyed a peaceful existence until in 1401 calamity struck the castle, when Owain Glyndŵr's men presumably destroyed it; the tragic finale for the castle has to be presumed because all future references to Painscastle in the records refer only to the town, which by that time had grown sufficiently to have developed a life of its own. Indeed the town of Painscastle prospered over the centuries and it is only in this twentieth century that life has begun to ebb away. When, in the next chapter, the towns of Radnorshire in the Middle Ages are under consideration, more will be said about Painscastle, and indeed about New Radnor too and Cefnllys, which will be visited next.

Llandrindod can rightly claim a number of cogent reasons why it should be visited; the author would like to cite an additional one, its proximity to Cefnllys, which is both a historical site of uncommon importance and also an area of outstanding natural charm. It lies a mile and a

half east of the town, via the Cefnllys Lane, an avenue of
desirable residences which gradually changes into a steep
and narrow lane, finally dropping down sharply to the
river Ithon, where the road ends. The Ithon runs only for
thirty-five miles, from its source five miles south of
Newtown to the spot a mile south of Newbridge, where
it feeds the river Wye, but in a great loop east of
Llandrindod it provided an extra defence for the
succession of strong points erected there. The centuries of
stirring historical events at Cefnllys were played out
along the banks of this stream between the Shaky and the
Alpine Bridges.

Let today's visitors park their cars and stand on the
Shaky Bridge and look north. On the west bank is a well-
planned nature trail, with a discreetly-appointed picnic
area close at hand, while across the meadow on the east
bank runs a footpath to the church, which is the only
building to be seen (GR 085615). Immediately above the
bridge to the east looms Cefnllys Hill, whose former
name Castle Bank explains the use to which earlier
visitors put the hill. To follow the chronological
development of early settlement here it is best to start at
the north end of the hill. To get there either walk along the
river bank to the Alpine Bridge or drive back to
Llandrindod, proceed eastwards along the A483 until the
road crosses the river Ithon at Llanbadarn Fawr, where a
sharp turning to the right along a minor road will after a
mile or so lead to the Alpine Bridge.

The seemingly isolated and uninhabited district
between the bridges for many centuries witnessed a
succession of human settlements of which the first had
been made on the Castle Bank itself at its north-eastern
end, where men and women of the Iron Age built their
simple huts, which they protected with earthen ramparts,

still to be seen on the side of the hill. Down below and quite close to the Alpine Bridge there is a mound (GR 092630), near the bank of the Ithon, which from early times could be forded at this spot. This mound, which is about sixteen feet high, lies about a mile north, north-east of St Michael's Church; it was thrown up between 1066 and 1086 by Roger Mortimer, whose men proceeded to add a wooden keep to the motte. This Roger was the first member of this influential Norman family to impinge upon the history of Radnorshire. The Mortimers, who came over from Normandy at the conquest, were kinsmen of William Fitz Osbern, whom William I had made Earl of Hereford after the battle of Hastings; twenty years later, when the Domesday survey was made, the Mortimers had acquired land in no fewer than eleven counties, with their main possessions in Shropshire and Herefordshire, where their chief seat, Wigmore Castle, had been built by Fitz Osbern himself. Cefnllys' first Norman castle (there were to be three of them) consisted then of a wooden tower, set on the flattened top of a mound on the river bank; a wooden fence built around this flat top will have afforded some protection to the bailey, where the soldiery lived. Little is known of the history of this first castle at Cefnllys beyond the fact that it was put up before 1086 and that it was still in use in 1104.

It is as well at this stage to stress the increasing importance of the impact of external events on the local history of the Marches; it has already been seen how Llywelyn ap Iorwerth, ruler of Gwynedd, in 1230 had been in a position to execute William de Braose, the Norman master of the castle of New Radnor, and how in the following year Henry III felt it necessary to visit Painscastle in person to make its defences more secure in

view of the probability of further attacks in the region by
the Welsh armies of Llywelyn. In 1242 the Mortimers,
faced with the rising tide of Llywelyn's military
successes, decided to build a new castle in Cefnllys on a
sturdier pattern and with more natural protection. Thus
Ralph Mortimer chose a site on the northern end of the
Castle Bank about a mile south of the previous motte and
bailey on the river bank; here, amid the surviving
earthworks of the Iron Age settlement, a stone castle was
built between 1242 and 1246. This new stone castle, which
consisted of a strong round keep, surrounded by an oval
bailey, enjoyed such protection as the river Ithon and the
steep cliffs of Castle Bank could afford.

All was well until 1255, when the Mortimers felt at
great risk in Cefnllys, because in that year, Llywelyn ap
Gruffudd, the grandson of Llywelyn ap Iorwerth (the
Great), became the Prince of Gwynedd and speedily
made himself master of much of Powys, where he
challenged the right of Henry III to hold down the
Marches. In the very next year the Welsh broke into open
revolt against the Crown, and in 1262 an armed band of
Welsh soldiers climbed up to the gates of Cefnllys Castle,
where they killed the porters and took prisoner the
constable; before leaving the hill, they set fire to the castle,
which they thereby put out of action. Soon Roger
Mortimer returned to the scene, camped with his soldiers
in the ruins and began to make the castle habitable again,
until Llywelyn ap Gruffudd appeared and drove him
away.

In 1267 hostilities between the Welsh and the English
came to a temporary halt when Henry III and Llywelyn
ap Gruffudd signed the Treaty of Montgomery, by one
clause of which Roger Mortimer was allowed to return to
Cefnllys, but whether this clause of the treaty permitted

him to restore the burned castle, as Llywelyn interpreted it, or allowed him to build a new castle on a different site, as Roger Mortimer chose to understand the matter, is open to some question. At any rate Roger Mortimer drew up plans to build a new castle on the other end of the Castle Bank, making good use of the building material available in the ruins of the burned castle. This new strong point, which was finished by 1274, consisted of a large tower, erected in the middle of a bailey, whose four corners were embellished with stout towers. It is also known that in 1282, the year in which Llywelyn ap Gruffudd died, Edmund Mortimer garrisoned Cefnllys Castle with eight cavalrymen and twenty infantrymen; the construction of this new castle was a sure sign of the English intention to maintain a strong presence in an important and disputed area. Throughout the thirteenth century Cefnllys played a crucial role in maintaining the authority of the English crown in the area, much clearing of neighbouring forests making communications much easier; in consequence it became safer for the English to travel in a wider area than previously. In the next century a succession of Mortimers continued effectively to maintain the English hold on the valley until quite suddenly a serious situation arose at the very beginning of the fifteenth century, when Owain Glyndŵr rose in revolt in North Wales. By 1403 Cefnllys Castle was again under attack, but, although defended by only twelve spearmen and thirty archers, they gave so good an account of themselves that the attack failed; the surrounding district, however, suffered severe devastation.

Cefnllys was now about to enter the last phase of its existence, when in 1425 Edmund Mortimer died, childless; seven years later the Crown appointed as Constable of the castle Ieuan ap Philip, who, by a timely rebuilding of some parts of the castle for a while, prolonged its useful life; in 1461, with the accession of Edward IV, Cefnllys passed into the direct possession of the King; Henry VII, who, as all Welshmen know, became King of England in 1485, eight years later gave Cefnllys Castle to his first-born son, Arthur, whose premature death in 1502 not only left Cefnllys without a custodian but exposed England to the tender mercies of his younger brother, the future Henry VIII, when his father died in 1509.

An interesting footnote to the history of Cefnllys Castle is provided by the comment of the sixteenth-century antiquary and historian, William Camden, who, visiting the area in the early 1580s, referred to the castle as a 'notable ruin'. Of the town of Cefnllys, which had grown up in the thirteenth century, under the castle at the foot of the hill and around St Michael's Church, something will be said in the next chapter. A postscript may here be justified in order to make mention of another Norman castle, remotely situated, whose vestigial remains may still attract the attention of the energetic connoisseur. It is the Castell Dinboeth (aka Dinbaud) GR 090754. It is to be found 1330 feet above sea level, about three-quarters of a mile NNW of Llananno, above the A483, before Llanbadarn Fynydd is reached. It now consists of little more than a deep ditch running round a substantial platform. Llywelyn ap Gruffudd destroyed it in 1260, and although it was later partially restored, it seems to have served no further useful purpose after Edward II in 1322 took it over from the Mortimer family.

## c. Norman towns

Readers will already have realised that around the three castles of New Radnor, Painscastle and Cefnllys towns of a sort gradually grew up to satisfy the needs of the garrisons there. This bare fact may have unwittingly caused a false inference to be drawn, namely that the Welsh peasantry in the respective neighbourhoods may have been forced to become the hewers of wood and drawers of water for their Norman masters. While the possibility of such happenings may not be entirely ruled out, for the most part the new towns were predominantly Norman settlements, where Norman immigrants were encouraged to settle in order to ply their various trades and to become important social and economic cogs in the Norman system of government. It is therefore very probable that beyond the limited areas where the Norman writ ran, most Welsh people in Radnorshire lived their separate lives as far as possible away from any Norman interference, with the result that two more or less separate communities, one Norman, the other Welsh, lived, probably near each other but with very little real contact. Of the three castle-towns, now to be described, New Radnor still survives – as a large village, Painscastle as a very small village and Cefnllys as quite deserted, save for the parish church.

The area below the castle at New Radnor was probably first settled shortly after 1096, when William II gave the castle to the de Braose family. From its creation as a borough in about 1096 until its devastation by Owain Glyndŵr in 1401, this little Norman town was besieged seven times and seven times suffered capture. It had been organised on a grid plan, as at Montgomery, its main streets being protected on three sides by earthworks and

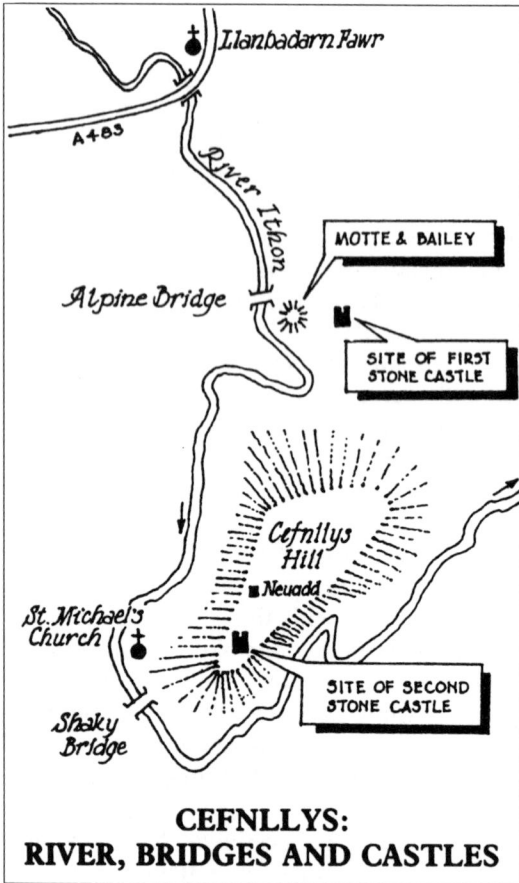

**CEFNLLYS:
RIVER, BRIDGES AND CASTLES**

ditches, traces of which are still visible. It was walled and
there were four gateways. New Radnor before 1401 was
in all likelihood entirely populated by non-Welsh people,
though the new town that was built thereafter had
primarily a Welsh population; this new town prospered
and, when in 1536 the Act of Union created the county of

Radnorshire, New Radnor became its first county town, despite the growing importance of two rivals at Knighton and Presteigne. New Radnor's superiority was further confirmed in 1562 when Queen Elizabeth granted their citizens a charter.

Today's visitors to New Radnor may ponder on the irony of the situation, as nothing remains of the medieval castle which gave rise to the need for a town, while the other source of authority in the Middle Ages, the parish church has altogether disappeared from view. Today's church is a Victorian building. Readers who may want to find out more about New Radnor and its neighbourhood are recommended to read W. H. Howse's books; he is the historian of east Radnorshire and he loved New Radnor dearly.

The town of Painscastle, as opposed to the castle, probably came into existence as a result of Henry III's rebuilding of the castle in stone in the summer of 1231, as the substantial garrison thereafter, stationed in the bailey of the castle above the village, came to require the services of many tradesmen, who will have built their homes in the village, where a town grew up sufficiently quickly in the thirteenth century for markets and fairs to be held there at least as early as in 1264. The days set apart for these important occasions were May 12th, September 22nd and December 15th. It is furthermore on record that in 1309 Painscastle possessed fifty burgesses. The centre of the town was, of course, the marketplace, which today is marked by a triangular patch of grass, just below the Maeswllch Inn. Visitors will look in vain for sign of a parish church, the nearest one being at Llanbedr, two miles westwards down the road towards the Wye valley. The absence of a church in Painscastle is to be explained by the probability that there was a garrison church at one time among the other stone buildings put up by Henry III on the hill.

The town seems to have survived, more or less unscathed, the disaster at the beginning of the fifteenth century when Owain Glyndŵr destroyed the castle. That it not only survived but continued to prosper was probably due to a happy geographical fact, namely that a number of drovers' routes from the heart of Wales passed through Painscastle, where the flock masters and their flocks found hospitality; there were at one time no fewer than six inns in Painscastle. There were also several forges in the district to attend to the weary feet of man and beast. In consequence the place became so busy that at one time the burgesses of the borough saw fit to petition, albeit unsuccessfully, for the right to be represented in Parliament.

The Victorian diarist Kilvert knew Painscastle well; readers are recommended above all to read the entry for July 3rd 1872, when he stopped awhile in the village and talked to a local farmer, who was also the elected mayor of Painscastle, an office which he ruefully explained had no emolument, no dignity and no powers! Today the school, opened in 1870, has become a community centre, the Post Office, whose opening Kilvert commented upon, has gone; closed too is the Congregational chapel down the lane under the castle, though a Baptist church still functions, along with the one surviving inn and a forge. An earlier visitor than Kilvert described Painscastle as 'an old and straggling Welsh townlet, with its great castle still dominating the narrow toruous streets, scene of a hundred bloody struggles, the Berwick of the southern Marches'.

The boundaries of the borough of Cefnllys, of which no sign above the ground is now at all visible, may be traced in the meadows around the church, where many a grassy hump still marks the site of a medieval home. The earliest reference to the town came in a market charter of 1297; this date corresponds with the approximate date for the building of the earliest part of the church. It was shown in the last chapter that in 1282 Edmund Mortimer, ten years after building the sturdy stone castle on a new site on the southern end of the hill, brought in a garrison, whose needs were from then on supplied by the inhabitants of the new town, which was growing up at the bottom of the hill.

There is a reference in a contemporary document to a toll, paid for crossing the bridge over the river Ithon, which presumably was at the stop where the Shaky Bridge is today. It is also known that in the course of the thirteenth and fourteenth centuries rents were paid by the burgesses to their masters on the hill for the privilege of farming some eighty acres. The borough, however, had a short and rather chequered existence; by the end of the fourteenth century its importance had undoubtedly dwindled, probably because it had come into being solely for the purpose of supplying a military settlement, whose importance too declined at about the same time. Nevertheless a few houses continued to be occupied down the centuries and it is known that in 1832, when the Boundary Commissioners visited the area, they reported that there were only sixteen burgesses, who lived in three farms and a cottage, all of whom enjoyed the right to elect a member to Parliament, a right which they were to have to relinquish.

St Michael's Church, though in a dilapidated state, continued to serve the lonely community until 1893, when the local archdeacon ordered its roof to be removed in order to compel the parishioners to attend the newly-

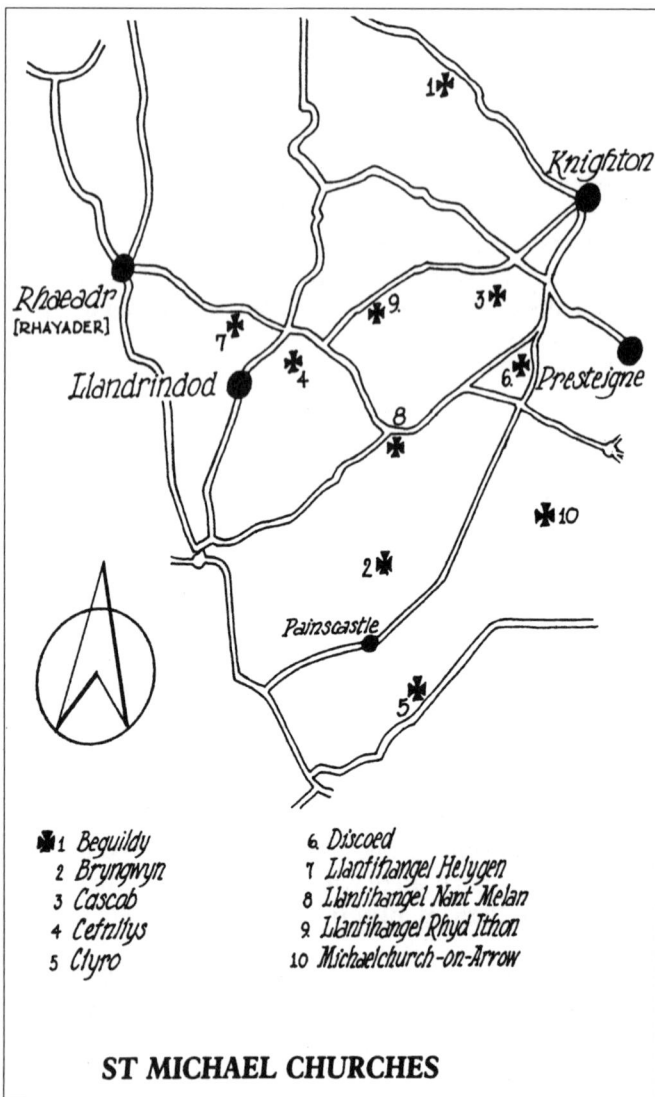

Knighton

Rhaeadr
[RHAYADER]

7

9

3

Llandrindod

4

6 · Presteigne

8

10

2

Painscastle

5

## ST MICHAEL CHURCHES

| | | | |
|---|---|---|---|
| 1 | Beguildy | 6. | Discoed |
| 2 | Bryngwyn | 7 | Llanfihangel Helygen |
| 3 | Cascob | 8 | Llanfihangel Nant Melan |
| 4 | Cefnllys | 9. | Llanfihangel Rhyd Ithon |
| 5 | Clyro | 10 | Michaelchurch-on-Arrow |

built Holy Trinity Church in Llandrindod. Public opinion, however, intervened and two years later Cefnllys Church was reroofed and services were resumed. St Michael's today has been sympathetically restored and is very carefully maintained; it stands in a circular churchyard, enclosed by ancient yews and its many summer visitors, who attend the services there, appreciate, it is to be hoped, the fourteenth-century font, the fifteenth-century screen and the seventeenth-century pulpit. All in all, this delectable of castle, borough, church and bridges is one of the true glories of Radnorshire.

### d. The Christian church in Norman times

It has already been seen how Christian missionaries in earlier centuries made their mark in Radnorshire, David, Teilo, Padarn and Cynllo establishing their llans, which in the course of time, if successful, became mother churches around which smaller religious communities sometimes grouped themselves. Some of these mother Churches became clasau, which were intellectual as well as spiritual centres. A number of these early religious settlements had survived into Norman times, some of them passing under Norman control. When this happened, the Norman pattern of church organisation, based on the authority emanating from Canterbury, was super-imposed upon the simple Celtic pattern. Such areas were divided into parishes, whose churches were then grouped together into dioceses, presided over by bishops, who, of course, were appointed by the Normans. In such circumstances former Celtic churches became Norman, and invariably their dedications were changed from Celtic missionaries to Roman saints, of whom in Radnorshire far and away the most commonly used were

St Mary and St Michael. This Norman reorganization into parishes and dioceses, under the supreme authority of Canterbury, was completed by the end of the twelfth century.

Some churches in Radnorshire, however, those which retained their Celtic dedications, escaped Norman overlordship; those were the churches dedicated to St David, Padarn, Teilo, Cynllo, Cewydd and Meilig. Of the dozen or so churches which still to this day enjoy Celtic dedications, a few still retain pre-Norman features and all are built in circular churchyards, which preceded by several centuries the rectangular shape favoured by the Normans for their churchyards.

The few early monasteries, the clasau already referred to, which had survived into Norman times, had lapsed by the twelfth century. The Christian church on the mainland of Europe had meanwhile produced a different form of monasticism several centuries before the Normans came to Britain. There were four main types of monastic orders, Augustinian, Benedictine, Cistercian and Dominician, but in Radnorshire only the Cistercians succeeded in establishing themselves, though there was for a while a Dominian cell at Rhayader. Of the fifteen Cistercian houses in Wales, the one in Radnorshire was at Abbey Cwm Hir (GR 056711).

Though only eight miles north of Llandrindod and five miles east of Rhayader, Abbey Cwm Hir is remote, far up a secluded valley, and even when the village is found, the remains of the abbey are becoming increasingly hard to discover. The Clywedog brook runs through the village, a fast-flowing tributary of the river Ithon; in a field next to this brook the Cistercian monks from Whitland Abbey built their new monastery in the middle of the twelfth century. As Cistercians at this time ate no meat, a river location was essential for a settlement, to ensure a supply of fish. Had the abbey ever been completed, it would have been the largest in Wales; as it was, its nave of two hundred and forty-two feet is only exceeded in length by the naves of Durham, Winchester and York.

The abbey seems to have flourished only in the thirteenth century, with its finest hour coming in 1282, when the body of Llywelyn ap Gruffudd, who had been killed in a skirmish near Builth, was carried to Abbey Cwm Hir, where it received honoured burial in front of the high altar. In 1401, during the troubled times of Owain Glyndŵr's rising, the monastery suffered seriously in a raid, while in 1542 its remaining buildings were dismantled in Henry VIII's Dissolution of the Monasteries.

At the lefthand side of the road that leads into the village, a public notice indicates a path that leads down the hill to the site of the abbey, several stretches of whose walls may still be seen, unless high summer has allowed nettles to encroach over them. In order to come upon the exact site of the high altar first look for a tree, in whose branches the remains may still be visible of metal wreaths, placed there in remembrance of the great Llywelyn, whose grave nearby is marked by a horizontal slab.

Visitors, who drive north from the village up narrow, hilly roads towards Llanidloes, should bear in mind that six complete arches from the abbey and most of the roof were carried over these steep hills to Llanidloes, where they were incorporated into the parish church, after a journey of quite extraordinary difficulty and devotion.

## e. Notes and Illustrations

### i. Motte and bailey

There is one particular motte and bailey above all others which readers are recommended to visit, if they want to identify with the logistics of life in Norman times. The Ordnance Survey map labels it (in gothic letters) Castell Crugerydd, while Giraldus Cambrensis, when he stayed there for two nights in 1188, refers to it as Cruker's Castle; its Grid Reference is 157593. It is situated off the A44, one and a half miles north-west of Llanfihangel Nant Melan; there is a convenient pull-in for motorists on the lefthand side, just before a hairpin bend. The choice of site reflects considerable credit on its architect, commanding as it does the Edw valley and overlooking a landscape, much favoured in even earlier times by settlers in the Bronze and Iron Ages. As the site has never been used since the original wooden keep and palisades fell victim to the joint ravages of time and weather, it is possible today to stand there (unless the wind is too strong!) and to recreate in the mind's eye what went on in this motte and bailey some nine hundred years ago and especially to imagine the scene when in 1188 Archbishop Baldwin and his scholarly interpreter Giraldus Cambrensis rode their horses up to the wooden castle.

### ii. St Michael

In the last chapter reference was made to the frequency of church dedications to St Michael; in all there are ten such churches in Radnorshire – Beguildy, Bryngwyn, Cascob, Cefnllys, Clyro, Discoed, Llanfihangel Helygen, Llanfihangel Nant Melan, Llanfihangel Rhyd Ithon and Michaelchurch-on-Arrow, in all, one in six of all churches in the county. The general tendency throughout England and Wales to dedicate churches to St Michael is worth further investigation. According to the Book of Revelations in the Bible, there was at one time war in heaven, when Michael fought against the dragon, whom Milton called Lucifer; eventually Lucifer was thrown out of heaven but he has been trying ever since to get back again, his favourite time for his annual attempt at revenge being thought to be at the end of September at Michaelmas, when the devil came to be associated in the public mind with equinoctial gales. Early Christians, who chose to personify the forces of good and evil, often dedicated their churches to St Michael, when they built them either on a hill or in hilly country, because they believed that a church so sited would be in a strong position for dealing with the powers of darkness, especially if they were in addition fortified by the dedication to St Michael. Readers may care to remember St Michael's Mount in Cornwall and across the Channel in France Mont S. Michel.

Although St Michael is the fourth most popular saint in church dedications in Britain as a whole, there are three times as many Michael dedications in Wales as there are in England, presumably because Wales is a hilly country. On the accompanying map, on which St Michael churches are marked, readers should note the proximity of five of them to the Radnor Forest, where men in former times believed a fearsome dragon lived; this belief reinforced the need for churches on the periphery of the Radnor Forest to welcome the extra help, which was thought to be theirs if their churches were placed under the protective patronage of St Michael.

### iii. Cascob

Cascob church (GR 239664), one of the St Michael churches, is worth exploring, although its village amounts to no more than the church, a farm, a superannuated school and a telephone kiosk outside the churchyard gates, where there is room for a car to park. This ancient site is today really remote, being seemingly built into the east flank of the Radnor Forest, above a long and narrow lane which runs for two miles westwards from the B4356. At this junction stands a group of Scots pine trees, which acted as route-markers until 1767, when by a re-routing by the Turnpike Trust the London to Aberystwyth Road no longer passed that way. The churchyard is very large and round; men and women may well have lived there before the first church was built, but whether these early squatters were Bronze people or later evacuees, who moved westwards to seek the security of the hills when the Romans left Britain, archaeologists have not yet been able to find out. Near the church porch are several large and very ancient yews, while inside the well-cared for church a curiosity will be found, hanging on the north wall, a framed parchment, which bears an Abracadabra charm, designed to drive out evil spirits that were believed to be troubling a parishoner three hundred years ago. The charm, which was dug up on the churchyard a few years ago, had probably been deliberately buried to gain extra potency for the invocation. Amidst this curious jumble of words, a mixture of English and Latin, will be found a quotation (unacknowledged) from the works of the great Elizabethan mathematician and man of magic, John Dee, whose family home was but a mile or two away from Cascob.

*Abbey Cwm Hir*

If Abbey Cwm Hir is approached from Crossgates via a finger-posted minor road off the A483 to Newtown, it is best to stop before the village is reached. Opposite the gates of the Hall a notice-board in the field above the river proclaims the existence of the abbey ruins, which may, with difficulty, be found down the path at the bottom of the hill. There is little enough left to see, but much to muse upon. There is more scope for reflection here than for photography.

In the middle of the illustration a gnarled tree marks the site of the high altar beneath which, in the place of honour, the headless body of Llywelyn ap Gruffudd was buried. A horizontal slab will be seen in the foreground, incised upon which is a cross and Llywelyn's name. If time allows, go on through the village (noting the remarkable inn sign of the Happy Union) and take the minor road westwards through wild and beautiful country to St Harmon.

*Castell Crugerydd*

This view of the motte and bailey is taken from a track to the south of the site. A walk to the top is recommended not only to study the lay-out of the bailey but also to enjoy the view of the Edw valley to the SW and of the Llandegley Rocks to the north.

*Cascob*

Here at the end of one of the most secluded and beautiful valleys in east Radnorshire stands St Michael's church, built on a small mound.

For nearly fifty years the 19th century vicar was the Rev. William Jenkins Rees, whose qualities and achievements are listed on a memorial stone in the chancel. He is the second of the three Radnorshire priests to be talked about later in this book.

# B. Developments in the twelfth and thirteenth centuries

## a. Giraldus Cambrensis in Radnorshire

The century-old confrontation between Norman Marcher lords and independent Welsh princes came to a temporary halt in 1170, when Owain Gwynedd, the ruler of Gwynedd, died, he, who had stood up manfully to all the attempts of Henry II to encroach further in North Wales. Thereafter, for a few years the strongest Welsh leader came from the South, where Rhys ap Gruffudd ruled the princedom of Deheubarth from Dinefwr Castle (near Llandeilo). From 1170 until the death of Henry II in 1189 there was an understanding between Henry II and Rhys ap Gruffudd, whom Henry always referred to as the Lord Rhys. During these unexpected years of cooperation a great military calamity in western Asia had a remarkable impact on the course of history in Western Europe. The military capture of Jerusalem and the Holy Places by the Mohammedan Saracens moved the Christian leaders in the west to take firm united action to right this affront to Christian civilisation. The result was the Third Crusade, wherein medieval men were able to indulge to the full their joint passions for fighting and praying in a common cause, which won great approval throughout Christian countries.

In London the Archbishop of Canterbury, Baldwin, who had succeeded the hapless Thomas à Becket, was authorised by Henry II to organise a journey through Wales to enlist recruits for the coming expedition to the east. Baldwin, who, despite his advanced age was to lead the journey in person (he died later, fighting in the Crusades), appointed as his interpreter and personal

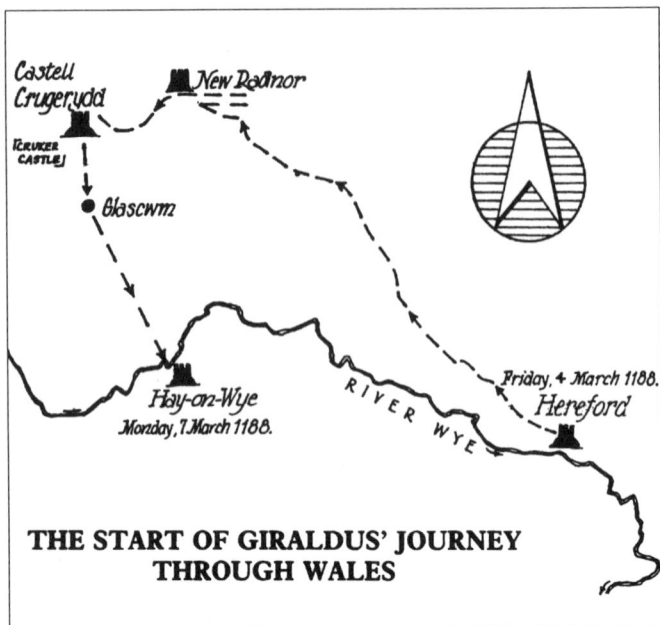

Castell
Crugerydd

[CRUKER
CASTLE]

New Radnor

Glascwm

Hay-on-Wye
Monday, 7 March 1188.

RIVER WYE

Friday, 4 March 1188.
Hereford

**THE START OF GIRALDUS' JOURNEY
THROUGH WALES**

chaplain a canon of St Davids, Giraldus Cambrensis, who
is today regarded as one of the outstanding personalities
of the twelfth century. This forty-year old cleric was part
Norman, part Welsh (he was a kinsman of the Lord Rhys),
well-born (in Manorbier Castle) and scholarly, (with great
ecclesiastical ambition). Early in March 1188 this
recruiting party rode out from Hereford.

On Ash Wednesday, March 2nd, the party, assembled
under the leadership of Archbishop Baldwin, attended
mass in the cathedral at Hereford, before two days later,
on Friday March 4th, setting out along the old Roman
road towards Kington (roughly speaking, the modern
A438); after passing through Kington (named after
Edward the Confessor), they rode out to New Radnor,

where they were to be entertained at the castle; they had ridden over thirty miles. New Radnor castle, readers will remember, was an important Norman frontier post on the boundary between Norman and Welsh lands. Waiting at the castle to greet Baldwin and his men was Lord Rhys, who had ridden over from Dinefwr Castle. Giraldus, in chronicling this fact, reminded his readers that Rhys was a close relation of his, whom he referred to as 'the Prince of South Wales'.

Courtesies having been exchanged and Baldwin's arrival duly announced to the neighbourhood, the Archbishop made the first of his many appeals in Wales for volunteers to take the cross. Hardly had he finished speaking than Giraldus, with a dramatic gesture, flung himself at Baldwin's feet and claimed the privilege of becoming the first Welshman to volunteer for the Third Crusade. This action, one gathers from reading Giraldus' later account of the episode, had been carefully planned in order to be accepted before his old rival, the Bishop of St Davids, who stood at his side and who was indeed the next to step forward and take the cross. Such volunteers, when found acceptable to the Archbishop, were given woven cloth crosses, which were stitched to the right shoulders of their coats, after they had been ceremonially blessed by the Archbishop. The business of the day thus satisfactorily concluded, the assembled company then had their supper in the castle before being entertained by Giraldus, who told them choice items from Radnorshire's real or imagined past.

Next morning the cavalcade moved on to Castell Grugerydd, which Giraldus called Cruker Castle; it was a short ride from New Radnor cross-country into the wild hill country of Radnorshire. Here, in the bleak landscape, where the wind was likely to have been keen in the first week of March, the party were to spend two nights. Clearly there had been much advance publicity, as many assembled there to listen to the Archbishop's pleading of his cause. Outstanding among the new volunteers was a cousin of Giraldus, Maelgwyn ap Cadwallon, the Prince of Malienydd (the northern part of Radnorshire). The adherence to the cause of this man of some substance was secured despite, in the words of his cousin, 'all the fears and lamentations of his family'.

Thoroughly rested, Baldwin and his retinue left Castell Crugerydd on Monday March 7th; their destination was Hay-on-Wye, in Brecknockshire, but before they reached Hay they probably passed through Glascwm (see map), an inference made from the fact that later that day after their arrival in Hay, Giraldus, in what was to become his usual fashion, enlightened his audience with stories and legends about the places seen earlier in the day, and on this particular evening Giraldus dilated upon the legends associated with Glascwm, which possessed the most ancient and important church in the area, one believed to have been founded by St David himself. The party, which then left Radnorshire, continued its journey through Wales in a clockwise direction, finally returning to Hereford on Saturday April 25th.

At the time of Baldwin's visit to New Radnor, early in March, the guardian of the castle was the infamous Norman villain William de Braose but, as he gets no mention in Giraldus' chronicle, it seems likely that he was away, living in one of his other castles, maybe Painscastle or more probably Abergavenny. In 1189, the year after the journey through Wales, Henry II died and was succeeded by his son Richard I. Confrontation between the Norman and the Welsh was immediately resumed. Rhys ap

Gruffudd returned to New Radnor but this time he came to lay siege to the castle, which he succeeded in capturing, in the process driving out de Braose; he also defeated a Norman army sent to try to win back the castle. Unfortunately for Welsh hopes, however, Rhys died the next year and before 1197 was out, de Braose was once again installed in New Radnor. The twelfth century ended in Radnorshire with Gwenwynwyn, the Prince of Powys, failing in his attempt to drive the Normans out of Painscastle.

## b. Llywelyn ap Iorwerth and Llywelyn ap Gruffudd

At the beginning of the thirteenth century the English grip on Wales seemed very secure, a state of affairs that was to be even truer at the end of the century, but, in the years between,Welsh hopes of independence were to run very high, largely through the exertions of two outstanding Welsh leaders, Llywelyn ap Iorwerth, and his grandson Llywelyn ap Gruffudd, sometimes tragically spoken of as the Last. It would be a distortion of the truth to pretend that, in this valiant struggle for Welsh independence in the thirteenth century, Radnorshire played anything other than a very minor role. There were however occasions in the lives of the two Welsh leaders when Radnorshire provided the stage for certain of their activities. These Radnorshire interludes will now be described but readers must be careful only to look at such events, when seen against the background of far more important developments elsewhere in the frantic Welsh effort to stay free from English rule.

The first of the two great leaders, Llywelyn ap Iorwerth, became prince of Gwynedd in the 1190s, and, after the death of Rhys ap Gruffudd, the Lord Rhys in

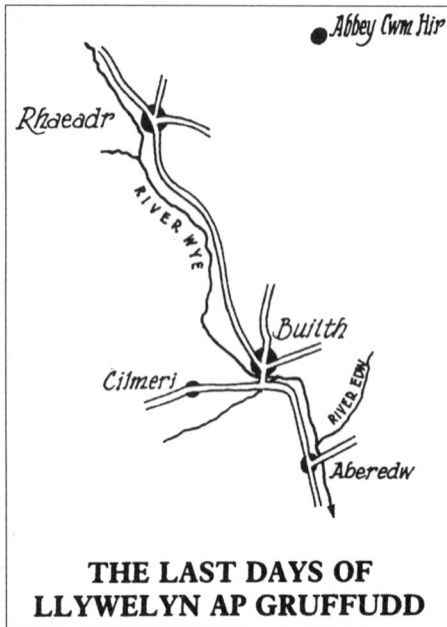

**THE LAST DAYS OF
LLYWELYN AP GRUFFUDD**

1197, became with Gwenwynwyn, the prince of Powys, the leading men in Wales. In the early years of the thirteenth century however John, who had succeeded his brother Richard I on the throne of England, took full advantage of the animosity and incompatibility that separated Llywelyn and Gwenwynwyn, and for a few years, in the time-honoured English way, divided and ruled. Nevertheless, by 1216, Llywelyn ap Iorwerth, at a gathering of Welsh princes at Aberdyfi, was acclaimed their leader and was given the title of the Great. For the rest of his life he used this authority to resist, wherever possible, any further encroachments by England, now ruled by Henry III, and in addition developed very considerable executive and administrative skills in organising the widely-differing territories under his command with a discerning eye to their future place in a unified and independent Wales.

New Radnor was the magnet that drew Llywelyn the Great to Radnorshire; in 1213, when the barons of England were in revolt against King John, Reginald de Braose, who had thrown in his lot with the dissidents, was helped by Llywelyn to capture New Radnor castle; shortly afterwards the victor married Llywelyn's daughter, Gwladys. After the signing of Magna Carta in 1215 peace was restored in England, occasioning Reginald de Braose to change sides and to support the new King, Henry III, who had succeeded his father John, in 1216. In 1230 Llywelyn was back in Radnorshire, and in the course of a highly successful campaign, in which he captured many an English stronghold in the Marches, he numbered among his conquests the castle at New Radnor, whose ruler was still Reginald de Braose, his son-in-law, whom Llywelyn proceeded to have put to death (in addition to changing sides Reginald was apparently suspected of seeking a liaison with Llywelyn's wife, Joan!). It was Llywelyn's capture of New Radnor castle in 1230 that prompted Henry III to spend the following summer of 1231 in nearby Painscastle, where he rebuilt the castle in stone and generally strengthened the defences of the area against any future attack by Llywelyn. Llywelyn, however, ignoring Painscastle, moved southwards and in 1233 in a surprise night attack captured Grosmont Castle, a powerful fortress a few miles north of Monmouth.

Seven years later, in 1240, Llywelyn, seemingly tiring of power, called an assembly of Welsh princes at Strata Florida (*Ystrad-fflur*) where he arranged for his succession before abdicating and retiring to a Cistercian monastery, where he died later in the same year. He must surely have believed that his successor would have been able to crown his father's achievement by obtaining full independence for Wales, whereas, with the benefit of hindsight, it can now be seen that the high-water mark of the Welsh attempt to win its freedom in the Middle Ages had coincided with the life and achievements of Llywelyn Fawr. His death, though followed by the agreed succession of his son Dafydd to the leadership of Gwynedd, led to fifteen years of fratricidal in-fighting; at Dafydd's death in 1246, three nephews contested the succession, which only resolved itself in 1255, when Llywelyn ap Gruffudd gained the better of his brothers and became prince of Gwynedd. Thereafter the struggle between Wales and Henry III was resumed, but the new ruler was in an unenviable position, with serious differences still dividing even his own family. In 1257 Henry took the offensive and indeed, for the next ten years, a fierce contest developed in which Llywelyn ap Gruffudd, against all the odds, stood out as a remarkably successful protagonist of the Welsh cause. Peace was signed by Henry III and Llywelyn at Montgomery in 1267, where the English king recognised his adversary as the Prince of Wales; for the five remaining years of Henry's life, Llywelyn ap Gruffudd was at his peak, with high hopes of achieving freedom for his people.

Henry III died in 1272, and with the accession of his son, Edward I, war at once broke out again between England and Wales, but in this critical and decisive moment in Anglo-Welsh relations cracks in the fabric of Welsh resistence widened ominously. Nowhere was this division more obvious or more serious than in Powys (of which, of course, Radnorshire was then a part). Unfortunately for Llywelyn's cause, Powys did nothing to help him and indeed many men of Powys actually chose to fight on the side of Edward I. This tragic development moved on to its even more tragic denouement, which brought Llywelyn ap Gruffudd on to the Radnorshire stage.

In the early winter of 1282 Llywelyn left his main troops in Gwynedd and moved south with a small force of men to try to regain lost lands in Powys and at the same time to recruit more volunteers for his armies. After detailing this small force to lay siege to Builth, which his enemies were holding on the west bank of the Wye, he slipped away to Aberedw, a few miles south of Builth, on the east bank of the Wye (and therefore in Radnorshire). Here, Llywelyn owned a castle in the woods high up on the south side of the village, where from time to time in the past he had come to enjoy some peace and quiet. In December 1282 he paid the castle a last visit, a visit which was soon brought to an end by the arrival of a message, pleading with him, for his safety's sake, to take shelter in a cave, a mile south-west of the castle. This cave may still, with some difficulty, be found (the Ordnance Survey map gives its exact location), though little enough remains to indicate where the castle once stood.

Legends and contradictory reports abound, concerning the last days of the great leader; it does seem likely that, while he was sheltering in the cave, a messenger came to him, inviting him to meet a Welsh deputation at an agreed rendezvous, west of Builth. Local tradition also insists that on the eleventh of December Llywelyn ap Gruffudd left his cave and went down to the village where he attended mass in Aberedw church, before setting out to meet his destiny. The most plausible sequence of events after leaving Aberedw church suggests that, after crossing the river Wye, he made his way west of Builth, where, in a field near Cilmeri, he stopped to slake his thirst in the river Irfon, only to be hacked down and killed by an English soldier, who was apparently unaware of his adversary's identity, until he searched the body and came across a sacred relic (allegedly a piece of the True Cross), which Llywelyn was known always to have with him. His identity thus established, the Englishman cut off his head and sent it to the King, while allowing his headless body to be taken to Abbey Cwm Hir, where the Cistercians gave it decent burial in front of the high altar.

The war with Edward in the north was to continue for another six months, but with the capture and subsequent execution of Llywelyn's brother, Dafydd, in Shrewsbury, the war came to an end and, with it, all hope of Welsh independence for another century and more, until, at the beginning of the fifteenth century, Owain Glyndŵr once again raised the banner of revolt.

To make sure that there could be no further renewal of Welsh political ambitions, Edward I in 1284 promulgated the Statute of Rhuddlan, whereby Gwynedd, the very heartland of Llywelyn's power and influence, was divided up into the three counties of Anglesey, Merioneth and Caernarfon. Furthermore, to ensure the military effectiveness of these arrangements, strong stone fortresses were built at Conwy, Caernarfon, Beaumaris and Harlech. In addition, the lands between the river Conwy and Chester became Flintshire, while in the south the two new counties of Cardigan and Carmarthen were set up. As far as 'Radnorshire' was concerned, it thereafter consisted of the private estates of Marcher Lords.

## c. Notes and Illustrations

### i. The siege of Llanbadarn Fawr church

In 1175 Giraldus Cambrensis, still under thirty years of age but already a distinguished graduate of the University of Paris and a much feared church disciplinarian, was made Archdeacon of Brecon by his uncle, the Bishop of St David's. The post had fallen vacant as a result of information given by the young zealot to his episcopal uncle concerning certain sexual misdemeanours of the incumbent archdeacon. Giraldus, soon after his installation at Llanddew, gave proof of a rigorous attitude towards the responsibilities of his office; accordingly, when word reached him of a lack of clerical rectitude in a remote part of his archdiaconate, he at once rode out, suitably escorted, in the direction of Llanbadarn Fawr in order to put things right.

His arrival at Llanbadarn (which is about two miles north-east of where today Llandrindod stands) was greeted by a hostile reception, which took the form of a shower of arrows, aimed at his party, which caused him, after stabling his horse in the churchyard, to seek refuge in the church; from this sanctuary he was able to despatch a messenger to his kinsman, Cadwallon ap Madog, who ruled that part of Elfael. Help was soon forthcoming, it seems, because, in the words of Giraldus, ' . . . the prince at once sent a sufficiency of victuals, with a message that he would come to him the next morning and take sharp vengeance on his wrongs, as if they were his own'.

Today's church, which is well worth a visit (it has a convenient car-park almost opposite) is little more than a hundred years old, but it stands in a circular churchyard, which speaks of the antiquity of the site. Furthermore, inside the porch above the south doorway, is a tympanum of quite remarkable quality, which, barely fifty years old at the time of the visit of Giraldus, will have looked down upon the agitated archdeacon, as he passed into the security of the church.

### ii. Glascwm's magic bell

At one time Glascwm is thought to have had in its keeping a much venerated possession, a handbell, which, according to tradition, had once belonged to St David, who is credited with having built the first church at Glascwm. Giraldus Cambrensis, in 1187, regaled his fellow-travellers, as they passed through Radnorshire in the early stages of the recruiting campaign for the Third Crusade, with a story about this ancient bell. In his own life-time, the story-teller went on, when the wife of a man, who was imprisoned in irons in the castle at Rhayader, heard about the bell's magical properties, borrowed the bell and took it with her to Rhayader, where she offered it to her husband's gaoler in exchange for his freedom. Her impassioned plea apparently fell upon deaf ears; the villainous gaoler seized the bell and proceeded to drive the poor woman away. However, as Giraldus told the story, God punished the evil-doer the very next night, by causing the castle at Rhayader to be burned down. In the conflagration only the bell survived and the wall on which it had been fixed. Tradition unfortunately offers no follow-up to these events; today we do not know if the prisoner escaped with his life nor is there any subsequent reference to what happened to Glascwm's magic bell.

*Llanbadarn Fawr*

It is perhaps hard to credit the wild happenings in the church just described. Today's church, practically rebuilt in 1878, still stands however in a circular churchyard and still has in its porch an early 12th-century tympanum and in its west wall an inscribed Roman stone, probably taken from nearby Castell Collen.

# C. A Welsh revolt and a Welsh Crown

The fourteenth century was a dismal time indeed for those Welshmen who still nurtured dreams of independence. With the benefit of hindsight however it can now be seen that, what appeared in the middle of the century to be a social calamity of the first order, helped to create a situation which in the long run gave Welsh, as well as English underdogs, a chance to flex their muscles. In 1348 and 1349 outbreaks of bubonic plague devastated a great part of the British Isles, resulting in the deaths of about a third of the entire population; the economic consequence of this disaster was a shortage of labour, which was to enable those peasants who survived the dreaded plague to demand a higher return for their labour. Hence in the second half of the century wages began slowly to rise, thus gradually improving the lot of the peasantry in Wales, as well as in England. English labourers, growing impatient at what they regarded as less than generous wage increases, broke into open revolt in the 1380s, an experience denied their fellow peasants in Wales. Hence, when the fifteenth century opened, social pressures were still building up in Wales, so that, when in the opening decade of the new century an opportunity for revolt presented itself, there were eager participants, waiting in the wings, ready and willing to play their part in Owain Glyndŵr's heroic adventure.

## a. Owain Glyndŵr in Radnorshire

If occasionally in this book it may have seemed that Radnorshire, in its happy remoteness, had figured mostly on the periphery of great events, the opposite  proved to be the case in the opening decade of the fifteenth century,

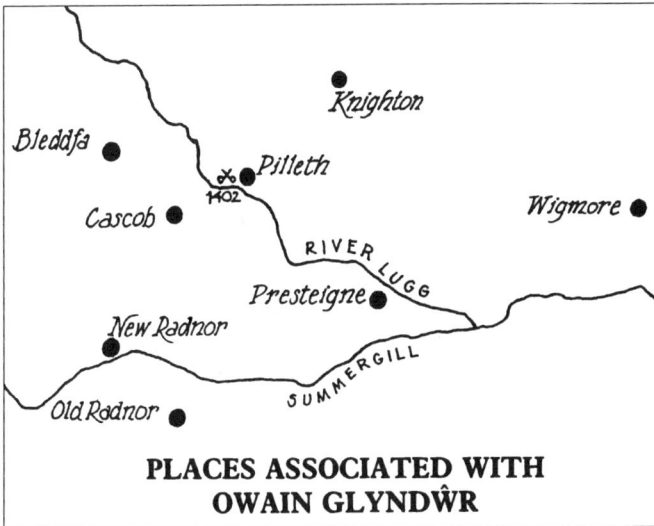

## PLACES ASSOCIATED WITH
## OWAIN GLYNDŴR

when a place in the Lugg valley, too tiny to be called a village, though it possessed a church, gave its name to a battle, which found its way into a Shakespearian play, but before this confrontation took place at Pilleth, it is necessary briefly to introduce the reader to Owain Glyndŵr, whose local territorial quarrel with Lord Reginald de Grey of Ruthin in 1400 merged into a war which within a year or two assumed quite gigantic proportions as a national struggle for the independence of Wales. Owain Glyndŵr was a forty-year old landowner, who had inherited one property in the Dee Valley between Llangollen and Corwen and another across the Berwyn Mountains in the Cynllaith Valley, south-west of Oswestry. It was there in 1400 that the first flames of revolt were ignited, when a dispute between Owain and Reginald de Grey of Rhuthun castle exploded into a war of independence against the English castles and boroughs which, for over a century, had been a central facet of the colonisation of Wales.

Owain was a man of breeding, a Welsh nobleman, with a lineage which included the *tywysogion* of Powys on his father's side and the *tywysogion* of southern Wales on his mother's side. He was also a poet, a lawyer and a soldier. However, during this time, the rights of the Welsh people were being sorely oppressed – whole areas were being ethnically cleansed to make way for English towns and castles. The Welsh were not allowed to hold office in their own country or speak their own language in the law courts. When the hour came, Glyndŵr was the natural leader.

On 16 September 1400, Owain was hailed Prince of Wales by an army of 300 of his followers at his court near Glyndyfrdwy. Two days later, they went on to attack Rhuthun, razing it to the ground on market day. In the ensuing years, every English town in Wales was burnt and a number of castles seized. Armies from England tried to extinguish the revolt, but they were defeated in a remarkable series of battles by Owain and his followers, and he became a master of guerilla tactics. At the height o his power, Owain established a parliament with representatives from every part of Wales, and he was crowned Prince of Wales in the presence of ambassadors from France and Scotland. The tide turned against him when England once again unleashed her full might to crush Wales, but Owain was never caught nor betrayed. He became a mythical figure, and his vision of an independent nation with its own church, university and parliament has been a template for modern Wales. This then is the background to the arrival in Radnorshire in 1402 of the army of Owain Glyndŵr.

Radnorshire had been marked out by Glyndŵr for

special attention, because its most important Marcher lord was Sir Edmund Mortimer; if his occupation of the castle at New Radnor could be broken, Glyndŵr reasoned, he would be able to march eastwards and attack the headquarters of the Mortimer family at Wigmore Castle in north Herefordshire, from where he dreamed of mounting an attack on the English midlands. As has been mentioned in an earlier chapter, the castle at New Radnor had passed into the possession of the Mortimer family in 1233, when Maud de Braose married Roger Mortimer. In 1402 armed bands of Glyndŵr's men roamed freely in eastern Radnorshire, wreaking havoc on the churches at Bleddfa, Cascob, Old and New Radnor, before uniting to drive Edmund Mortimer out of his castle at New Radnor, whose entire garrison of sixty men was put to the sword. All this was but preparation for a full-scale engagement with Mortimer's army, which Owain Glyndŵr planned for the summer of 1402.

Readers who want to identify more closely with the battle of Pilleth (GR 257683) are recommended to use the B4356, which runs north-west from Presteigne. At the spot on the map where Pilleth is marked, a finger post will be found north of the road, indicating the approach to the church. This is only a bumpy, grassgrown track but is wide enough for a car (though most certainly *not* for a coach); suitable parking is available near the church in a clearing under Bryn Glas.

Hereabouts, late in June 1402, Glyndŵr's men waited on the hillside as the army of Edmund Mortimer marched towards them along a track, which ran round the hill, from a south-easterly direction. Welshmen in numbers were present in both armies, but as these armies closed, the Welsh bowmen of Owain Glyndŵr quickly gained the upper hand over Mortimer's men, and soon a great many of Mortimer's Welsh levies changed sides. The battle soon became a rout in which a thousand men of Mortimer's army were slaughtered.

Visitors to the site today should make a point of scanning the hill to spot a clump of redwoods, which were planted in after years to mark the graves of those who perished in the battle. Note too the well in the churchyard, just north of the church, where thirsty soldiers came to quench their thirsts on that bloody summer morning. News of this rather one-sided contest reached the King's ears in London, where, in the first Act of Shakespeare's play, *Henry the Fourth Part I*, the Earl of Westmoreland is made to break the news to his royal master in these words.

' . . . but yesteryear there came
A post from Wales loaden with heavy news;
Whose worst was that the noble Mortimer,
Leading the men of Herefordshire to fight
Against the irregular and wild Glendower
Was by the rude hands of that Welshman taken,
A thousand of his people butchered.'

As footnote to this bare bulletin it has to be added that 'the noble Mortimer', taken prisoner in the battle, also changed sides and subsequently married one of Owain Glyndŵr's daughters and became Glyndŵr's right-hand man in his bid to free Wales from English rule!

Glyndŵr's triumph at Pilleth represented a watershed in the fortunes of the uprising; the way ahead thereafter beckoned to him, as a revolt in the Marches burgeoned into a full-scale war for national independence, at a time when his enemy, Henry IV was grievously beset by problems both at home and overseas. The only immediate check suffered by Glyndŵr was provided by the King's son, the future Henry V, who, while Owain Glyndŵr was lighting the fires of independence up and down the country, marched north from Monmouth and burned down Glyndŵr's two homes, at Sycharth and Glyndyfrdwy.

By the end of 1404, Glyndŵr's year of triumph, he had set up a national parliament at Machynlleth, where a blueprint for a future independent Wales was debated and agreed; a free Wales was to have two universities, a civil service was to be created, whose members would all speak Welsh, and the Welsh church was to be removed from the jurisdiction of Canterbury. Alas for the hopes of Glyndŵr's supporters, Henry IV, after sorting out his domestic problems and dealing successfully with his enemies in France and Scotland, was free to use his armies against the Welshman, who by the end of 1410 had lost all the lands he had previously gained. Henry IV proclaimed him an outlaw and after 1412 no man ever saw him again, no-one knowing when or where he died, though there is a strong likelihood that he ended his days in a remote part of Herefordshire, in the Golden Valley, in the home of one of his daughters who had married a Scudamore. This great leader nevertheless had kindled a flame, which has never been put out in the hearts and minds of many Welsh people.

## b. The Tudor advance

The fifteenth century, which had dawned so brightly for Welsh hopes of independence, soon went sour, as rigorous repression followed the failure of Glyndŵr's rising. Though in fact the terrible penal code, enacted by Parliament, under Henry IV, was rarely applied after his death in 1413, yet its very presence on the Statue book did much to feed the bitterness of disappointed Welshmen. The first half of the fifteenth century was then a bleak time for Welsh hopes and nothing happened anywhere in the country to dispel the gloom. In the second half of the century, however, momentous changes were afoot, which, though they took place mostly in England – and not at all in Radnorshire – yet were destined to affect the lives of all Welshmen, as well as of all Englishmen too. The patience of readers has here to be sought, because without even a telescoped survey of these developments, it is not possible to understand the continuity of history in the Marches at this time.

In the middle of the century the long-drawn out Hundred Years War with France came to an end, and in consequence a great many soldiers were brought back from the continent, soldiers for whom new tasks were soon to be assigned. It is perhaps relevant here to mention that in the various armies, gathered together for service in France, there had been very many Welshmen, for whom in the current economic circumstances no other jobs had been available. Readers of Shakespeare's historical plays will remember, particularly in *Henry V*, the parts played by Welsh soldiers, like Fluellen.

The most complicated drama in the whole of English history was about to be enacted in the second half of this century, just when there were enough soldiers, freed from other commitments, to play the leading roles. Rivalries between two families, both with strong claims to the throne, bedevilled life in England, and in Wales, from 1460 to 1485; on the surface this struggle appeared to be local, in so far as it concerned the claims of Yorkists and Lancastrians, whereas in fact Wales had never found itself before so involved in a seeming alien contest. This strange situation will be readily understood, when it is realised that a leading Welshman was for some time the chief adviser to the Yorkist command, while the Lancastrian claimant to the throne was himself a Welshman, Henry Tudor. Wales was more or less equally divided in its loyalties, with Radnorshire, comprising the homeland of the Mortimer family, espousing the Yorkist cause, and the north, north-west, west and south-west for the most part proving loyal to the Lancastrians.

Who this Henry Tudor was and what were the circumstances that enabled this well-born Welshman to claim the crown not of an independent Wales but rather of England are questions that have now to be answered. Since the early years of the thirteenth century the Tudor family, who lived in North Wales, had supported the rulers of Gwynedd, one of their number having been steward to Llywelyn ap Iorwerth; thereafter the Tudors grew in power and acquired considerable estates, especially in Anglesey. In the recent uprising members of the Tudor family had supported Owain Glyndŵr, being his cousins, and in consequence suffered in the subsequent reprisals, one of them only succeeding in achieving eminence and that in a memorable way. Glyndŵr's nephew, Owain, christened thus in honour of his illustrious uncle, became, to the puzzlement of many Welshmen, after the death of Henry IV, page-boy, with his name anglicized to Owen, at the English court of the youthful Henry V, the victor of Agincourt. This puzzlement must have turned to consternation when, after the early death of Henry V in 1422, his twenty-year old French widow, whose infant son had become Henry VI, married the former page-boy, Owen Tudor. The marriage prospered and produced four children, one of whom, Edmund, later the Earl of Richmond, in the fulness of time married Lady Margaret Beaufort, the great great grand-daughter of Edward III; their son, Henry, by virtue of the relationship he had acquired with Edward III, becoming the Lancastrian claimant to the throne of England.

The Wars of the Roses broke out in 1460, and within a year the Yorkists had won the Battle of Mortimer's Cross, a few miles to the east of Presteigne, but just over the border in Herefordshire; the victor was the head of the pro-Yorkist Mortimer family, who then became King of England as Edward IV. With his accession, the Lancastrian cause was in disarray, ten years later necessitating the removal of the fourteen-year old Henry Tudor to a safe exile in France, where he would have to await a change of fortune, which would enable him to return to make good his claim to the throne.

This long-awaited day dawned in August 1485, when on the 7th the twenty-eight year old Henry Tudor stepped ashore in Pembrokeshire at the head of a large army, which was to swell the further he marched into Wales. Four days later Henry arrived in Machynlleth, where a change of route took the invaders eastwards along well-marked drovers' routes towards Shrewsbury, which was reached on August 15th. Exactly a week later the Lancastrian army under Henry clashed with the army of Richard III on the Field of Bosworth, with results that all men know. The victorious Henry thereafter marched to

London, where Parliament welcomed him and accepted him as Henry VII, King of England. Thus it was that a Welshman became the King of England, but Wales did not thereby become a part of England. What in this book, for the sake of clarity, has so far always been referred to as Radnorshire (in the hope that today's readers in Radnorshire might the more readily be able to identify with their past history) from the Conquest until 1485 was a part of the Marcher lands, which were so designated after the Conquest to indicate territories given to favourite Norman lords by the King; various families, of which the Mortimers were probably the most important, held sway in Radnorshire. These local leaders in the Marches – and the Mortimers were certainly no exception – often took the law into their own hands and ruled more like independent monarchs than infeudated vassals of the King. In an attempt to bring the Marcher lands back under the direct control of London, Edward IV, a few years previously, had set up in Ludlow a Council of the Marches, but it seems to have achieved very little. Henry VIII, in his reign from 1485 to 1509, tried to increase direct control over the Marches by reviving Edward IV's Council and indeed sent his eldest son, Arthur, to Ludlow to act as a sort of viceroy, but after his untimely death in 1502, his successor, the future Henry VIII chose never to visit Ludlow. In other words, the presence of a Welshman on the throne of England made no obvious difference to the way the Marcher lands were governed.

If Henry VII disappointed Welshmen by doing too little to improve the way in which Wales was governed, his son, Henry VII more than made up for it in the Act of Union 1536, when for reasons probably quite unconnected with the needs or the welfare of Wales, he caused sweeping changes to be made. The very title of the act, however, was most misleading, resembling as it did a peace treaty made at the end of a war and dictated by the victor.

The Marcher lordships were all abolished and in their place new counties were created, of which Radnorshire was one; these counties thereafter elected members of parliament to Westminster. English law – and English law alone – was to be adhered to in Wales, despite the vast body of Welsh law that had accumulated since the time of Hywel Dda. In every county new courts of law were set up to deal with less serious crimes; these courts were to be presided over by Justices of the Peace, a system that had worked satisfactorily in England since the fourteenth century. Those JPs, who became responsible for the maintenance of law at this lower level and indeed for the whole administration of local government, operated in Quarter Sessions, which were to meet four times a year. For more serious crimes, like murder and robbery, higher courts were established, Wales being for this purpose divided up into four circuits, which Judges visited twice a year. These higher courts, the so-called Great Sessions of Wales lasted until 1830.

Thus far the new legal system seemed a fairer one than Wales had known before – at least there was now uniformity which had hitherto been lacking. Bitter and long-lasting resentment, however, were felt at the insistence that in all the courts of Wales, be they the Quarter Sessions or the Great Sessions, only the English language was allowed to be used. This proviso was exceedingly unjust as it prevented many a Welsh defendant, who knew only his own language, from understanding what was happening around him. Furthermore, as a consequence the Welsh language went into a steep decline, because the rapidly-developing

Welsh middle class, who sought social advancement, hastened to learn English in order as soon as possible to qualify as Justices of the Peace at Quarter Sessions. One other provision of the Act of Union which concerned Radnorshire, created in Ludlow an expanded form of the Coucil of the Marches, to be known as the Council of Wales, which then became the centre of Welsh government.

*Pilleth Church*

St Mary's church has twice been the victim of fire, the first time in 1402, the second in 1894, when the roof of the nave was destroyed.

### The Well
### in Pilleth Churchyard

Famous in the Middle Ages for the relief its waters gave to those with eye trouble. In June 1402 battle-scarred soldiers slaked their thirsts there.

### Redwoods at Pilleth

Three redwoods were planted on Bryn Glas, above the churchyard, to commemorate those who died in the battle there in June 1402.

# III. After 1536

Up to now, a more or less chronological approach has been adopted in this book, which will now be abandoned in favour of a more topical method. Topics chosen will be of national Welsh importance as well as being of particular relevance to Radnorshire, where a great deal of visual evidence survives, which will enable the enthusiast to search out and identify the bare bones of history! Such an approach should be especially rewarding in considering the first of these topics, the Drovers' Routes, because a number of them crossed the county on their way eastwards to markets in England.

## 1. The Drovers' roads

Radnorshire is a living history book, one vivid chapter of which is concerned with these Drover's Roads, whose presence is revealed in the location of Drovers' Inns and Cider Houses, as well as the clumps of well-placed Scots pine trees, about which more will be said later. First however these roads must be put into their historic Welsh setting.

From the early Middle Ages Welsh farmers bred cattle, mostly of the sturdy black variety, to which the distant lowlands of England offered a substantial and enduring market, if only the beasts could be brought to the customers. To take full advantage of an expanding market, Welshmen learned how to drive their cattle great distances to the east. In the course of time a pattern emerged, as local herds in different parts of Wales congregated at agreed places where the animals were organised for the long journey out of the country; droves were generally subdivided into sections of about four

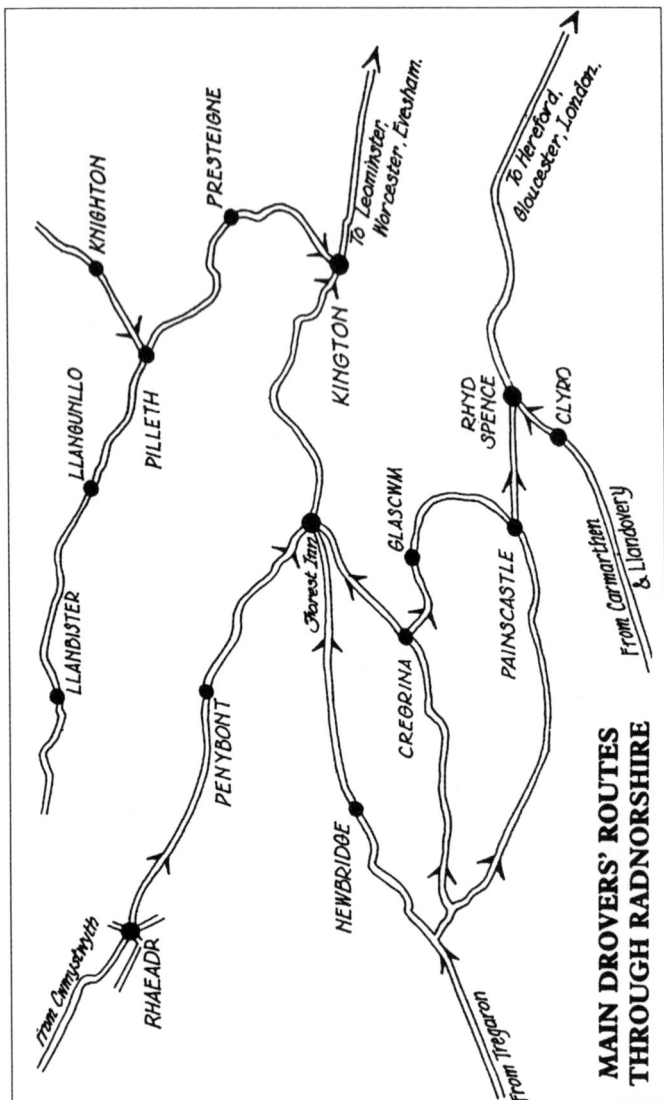

MAIN DROVERS' ROUTES
THROUGH RADNORSHIRE

hundred head of cattle, for whose welfare up to twelve men were responsible. While most drovers had to go on foot, the drovers' leaders rode on ponies, which, after the mission was completed, they normally sold for good prices in England, before starting out on their long, leisurely trek home on foot to Wales. Of quite invaluable assistance to the drovers were their corgi dogs, who were chosen for their speed, tenacity and intelligence. Many were the stories told about the speed shown by these dogs in finding their own way home after their masters had sold their cattle. In one area, folk memory asserts, women regarded the reappearance of their corgis as proof that their husbands would show up within the following two days!

Any accurate estimate of the number of cattle in a convoy is hardly possible, but sundry facts have emerged from local records, which give some idea of the size of this outstandingly important trade. For instance in the seventeenth century three thousand cattle a year left Anglesey en route for the English market, a number which by the following century had trebled; in this same eighteenth century it is known that thirteen thousand cattle passed through Herefordshire every year and something like twenty thousand head annually left Pembrokeshire.

Before the annual take-off of the droves of cattle, which in the course of time came to include sheep, pigs and geese, all the creatures' feet had to receive adequate protection, different animals needing different types of footwear; the shoes with which the black oxen were shod were known as cues (in Welsh ciw) and provided Welsh blacksmiths with much winter employment and strong men with considerable exercise, when the actual shoeing took place. A cue consisted of two thin pieces of iron, which were nailed over the cloven hooves, but first the ox had to be captured, usually by having a rope thrown round its neck by one man, while another man pushed it to the ground, where its legs were tied together, thus making it possible for the smith to fix the iron plates, eight to a beast. These cues had to be renewed again and again in the course of the long trek eastwards, hence forges were built at strategic points along the drovers' routes, generally near the inns.

In modern times naval convoys travel at the speed of the slowest ship, and so it must have been with the droves of cattle; a speed of two miles an hour is thought to have been average. A few records have survived of times taken for actual journeys; for instance, the time taken for a drove from Tregaron via Radnorshire to Warwickshire was sixteen days, while five days more were required by drovers who had to take their cattle from north Wales to Kent. There are a number of marginal references to cattle droves in contemporary literature, all of which comment on the enormous noise which could be heard several miles before any visual sighting was made. These long journeys must often have been very dangerous, especially as wolves roamed the uplands of Wales until well into the eighteenth century and highway robbers were still active on these routes at a much later date. It has been suggested that considerable clearance of trees and shrubs were made at various places in Wales to deprive the brigands of suitable lookouts and hiding places.

The drove masters, bestriding their ponies, had much to arrange; the chief expenses incurred were for cattle food, hay and grass, food and lodging for the large number of men who attended to the animals, and for the renewal of the animals' footwear. Many of the ancillary workers will probably have slept rough but their masters will all have insisted on accommodation indoors. The pay of the drovers in general was considered good, compared with the wages of others who worked on the land.

Blacksmiths, innkeepers and farmers, who were prepared to offer bed and breakfast accommodation, certainly welcomed the arrival of the drovers. Traditionally in Wales Scots pines had often been planted for specific purposes, in early times such trees being used to mark routes in remote country; this Welsh association with these distinctive trees was renewed by farmers on the drovers' routes, when they wanted to advertise their bed and breakfast accommodation for the drovers by planting clusters of these Scots pines.

The droving trade which had grown up and developed in a haphazard fashion expanded in the sixteenth century at a time when by the Act of Union the English government had made itself responsible for the administration of Welsh affairs. In consequence the trade soon became regulated by statute; thanks to acts of Parliament in the reigns of Edward VI and Elizabeth, drovers had to be officially licensed. This licence they had to apply for every year, to qualify for which a man had to be at least thirty years of age, married and the owner of a house. In the following century drovers found their livelihood threatened by the outbreak of civil war in the 1640s, but once the war clouds had passed, there was very considerable expansion in the trade with the number of cattle crossing into England greatly increasing from year to year; by this time famous English country houses were placing regular orders with the drovers to supply them with sufficient cattle to enable them to satisfy their guests' appetite for the 'roast beef of old England'!

Two events in the eighteenth century made significant

changes in the lives of drovers. Firstly, as Nonconformity spread in Wales, the sanctity of the Welsh sabbath was stressed, causing all drovers to stay where they were on Sundays; this sanction was strictly enforced and the financial penalty suffered by occasional defaulters was extremely heavy. Again, in the second half of the century, when turnpike roads came into existence and toll-gates were erected, the charges of the latter appeared so preposterous to the drovers that they took their cattle off the roads and made their own tracks towards England over hill and dale.

By the eighteenth century leading drovers were not only men of some substance but of an assured position in their society; at a time when the roads of Wales were few and bad and hence little used, the drovers, thanks to the nature of their job, travelled far and wide, meeting people from other walks of life, with whom they exchanged opinions and discussed the news. It is said that it was a drover returning home in the summer of 1815 who first brought to his home district news of Napoleon's defeat at Waterloo. Drovers frequently acted as letter carriers, maintaining contact between parents in Wales and sons in England, maybe following the law in London or studying in English universities, to whom welcome sums of money were brought from Wales.

It was perhaps above all for the financial role they performed that drovers assumed such importance in later days, because frequently they were entrusted with large sums of money in Wales, with which they were asked to pay off debts in England incurred by their employers. In such cases most drovers, fully aware of the dangers of being attacked by robbers on their journey, deposited the money in banks in Wales before setting out. Later they settled these debts in England by using the money they received from the sale of their cattle. Indeed drovers did much to encourage the growth of private banks in Wales, one of the best known of which was founded by a drover in Llandovery in 1799, the Black Ox Bank; this drover, David Jones had by 1820 become so prosperous that he was made High Sheriff of Carmarthen, and in Radnorshire at about the same time another successful drover, Evan Davies by name, also became High Sheriff of the County. By then the day of the drover was nearly over because the advent of the railways in the early nineteenth century brought his long and useful career to a sudden end.

The accompanying diagram will give some idea of the inroads made by drovers' routes in Radnorshire; only the most-used of these routes have been marked here but, in fact, many droves of cattle were taken over the hills and through byways, passing through remote villages. Four of the busiest routes in the whole of Wales, however, did pass through the county, those from Cwmystwyth, Strata Florida, Tregaron (over the incomparable Abergwesyn Pass) and from Carmarthen (via Llandovery).

Glascwm, south of the Forest Inn, is specially recommended for a visit; it is today a delightful but exceedingly quiet settlement, which was at one time far busier than it is now, its bustling importance being entirely due to the frequent passage through the village of the drovers, for whom accommodation was available in several inns. A further amenity, put at the disposal of the drovers and their assistants, was a race course. All trace of these days has gone but a visit is well-worth while, especially if it is followed up by a short drive along green and narrow lanes to Painscastle, which was situated at a point where several drovers' routes joined up. In Painscastle, opposite the one surviving drovers' inn is a forge, where in other days many a herd of black cattle received new cues.

## 2. 17th Century: local impact of Civil War and the Commonwealth

In 1642 stresses in the body politic, which had been growing alarmingly in the previous decade, brought about civil war, with Parliament in London taking up arms against their King, Charles I. In the ensuing struggle, which was to culminate in 1649, when Parliament executed the King, the country was seriously divided, in some parts village fighting against village, with even members of families being on opposite sides; in Wales however such fundamental differences were largely avoided, as the issue seemed to be more clear cut. The injustices, implicit in the Act of Union sixty years before, had not yet manifested themselves to the majority of Welsh people, who in 1603, when James I came to the throne, had transferred their loyalty without any qualms from the Tudors to the Stuarts.

In 1642, most of Wales supported the royal cause, south Pembrokeshire and the castles of Chirk and Ruthin in the north of the country, where Sir Thomas Myddelton held sway, almost alone supporting Parliament in the early days of the conflict. The bulk of Welsh support came from the gentry and the middle class, which had benefited most from the Act of Union, but there were very many Welshmen in the ranks of the regular army, who were to fight for the King at Edgehill and Naseby. In England the growing Puritan movement did much to buttress the Parliamentary cause but in Wales at this time there were as yet very few Puritans and little enthusiasm for their beliefs.

Such was the general position in Wales; in Radnorshire however the attitude towards the King was far more sympathetic than elsewhere, stemming in all probability from a widespread personal affection for Charles I, who from his youth onwards had been in the habit, whenever possible, of spending his leisure time on an estate in Radnorshire, between Evenjobb and Presteigne, which his father, James I had given him; here he hunted and indulged in other country pursuits. In the 1630s when the King had been very seriously embarrassed by financial problems, he had sold a part of his Radnorshire estate, but apparently some of the tenants of the new owners clubbed together and bought back the former royal property and presented it to Charles.

When in 1642 the King set up his headquarters in Shrewsbury, he sent the young prince of Wales, the future Charles II, south into Wales, where he passed through Radnorshire; his task was to whip up enthusiasm for the royal cause, a mission which seems to have been especially successful in Radnorshire. The first military action in the civil war in Radnorshire took place in October 1642, by which time Hereford had already been seized by parliamentary forces. When news of this royal loss reached Presteigne, some twenty-six miles away, leading local royalists foregathered, under the leadership of the displaced MP for Hereford, Charles Price, the MP for Radnorshire. After decisions were taken to organise an attempt to recapture Hereford, the party adjourned to a nearby hostelry, where their pleasures were interrupted by a band of soldiers sent down from Hereford, who proceeded to round up as many royalists as possible, including Charles Price himself, who was forced to march to Hereford with them. He was later allowed to return to Presteigne, where two years later he was stabbed to death in a street in Presteigne by a parliamentary soldier. In that same year of 1644 there was some more military activity, this time in remote Abbey Cwm Hir, where an enthusiastic group of Royalists turned the ruins of the abbey into some sort of a fortress from which they were ejected by a band of Parliamentary troops. The royal garrison surrendered, comprising several officers and sixty to seventy soldiers; later on in 1644 fighting in the civil war in Radnorshire came to an end when another Parliamentary force drove the Royalists out of the castle at New Radnor before finally reducing the old fortress to utter ruins. In this campaign generally as the Royalist cause lost battles, so it lost support, even in Wales. The military climax came in 1645, when the King lost the battle of Naseby, prompting most Welshmen thereafter to change their allegiance. Naseby had been fought on June 14th; between then and the royal defeat outside the walls of Chester on September 24th, Charles twice passed through Radnorshire.

Extricating himself from the Naseby disaster, the King straightaway moved south-westwards to Hereford and from there to Cardiff, his purpose to rally support for the cause and to recruit more men. At the beginning of August he set out on his whirlwind return journey, this time passing through Brecknockshire and Radnorshire; on August 7th he crossed the Wye into Radnorshire at Glasbury, where he was duly met by the Lord Lieutenant. From there he climbed with his party up steep and narrow lanes from Erwood to Painscastle, and from there via Rhos Goch, Newchurch and Gladestry to spend the night in the parish of Old Radnor. The modern B4594 road, traverses the same route. The night was spent in a small farm, Bush Farm off the modern B4357; tradition asserts that Charles, having spent the night in the farm with his famished party, changed its name in the morning to Beggar's Bush (GR 263643). (An incident that occurred on the day's march from Glasbury to Beggar's Bush will be described in the fourth section of this chapter under Notes and Illustrations.) The next day the royal party arrived at Ludlow, the whole journey from Cardiff to Ludlow having taken only three days. The King arrived back at his headquarters in Oxford on August 28th.

The second visit to Radnorshire in 1645 began when the King left Oxford on August 30th en route for Hereford, which he left on September 18th; after a march which lasted from six o'clock in the morning until midnight, Charles spent the night near Presteigne, probably at Lower Heath, two miles south-east of the town. Here he spent a second night before taking to the road again; travelling via Knighton and Newtown he reached Chester, where at the battle of Rowton, fought under the very walls of the city, the royal cause suffered irreparable losses on September 24th. Events thereafter seem, with the benefit of hindsight, to have moved inexorably towards the final scene on the scaffold in London in January 1649. It is perhaps a sad commentary on the change of Welsh loyalties at this time that two of those who signed the King's death warrant were Welshmen.

With the war ended and the monarchy brought to a sudden end, Parliament found itself faced with a number of critical problems. As an answer to one of these problems Parliament decided to initiate a policy of fostering the spread of Puritanism in Wales; indeed Oliver Cromwell had already settled some of his soldiers in Radnorshire with this policy specifically in mind. Over and apart from this parliamentary policy of spreading dissatisfaction with the reformed church as established by the Reformation, there had been for some time a growing awareness among Welsh people that the Protestant reformation had not gone nearly far enough in breaking with the past. From the time of John Penry (the undersung hero of Welsh Puritanism, who died for his Puritan beliefs as early as 1593) many had seen the need for a more fundamental change in the church in Wales in order to cater for the needs of ordinary Welsh people.

In 1650 Parliament passed the Act for the Better Propagation of the Gospel in Wales, to implement the findings of which Colonel Thomas Harrison appointed seventy commissioners whose task it was to tour Wales and to eject from their livings those whom they thought to be unsatisfactory priests; in the three years of its existence (the Act was ended in 1653) more than three hundred Welsh priests were dismissed. In the absence of suitable replacements a system of itinerant preachers was established, foremost among whom in Radnorshire was Vavasor Powell (about whom more will be said later). Despite the work of outstanding preachers like Powell, this itinerant system was quite inadequate in supplying the needs of the people. Perhaps in consequence, at this time a number of new Christian sects came to life, each of which tended to interpret the Bible in its own distinctive way. Even so there was no very great upsurge of Puritanism in the county under the Commonwealth. Indeed, when Cromwell, growing impatient with his parliaments, dispensed with them and made himself Lord Protector, many dissident preachers rose up against him. Welsh attitudes towards Oliver Cromwell began to harden and when in 1660 the monarchy was restored in London there was as much rejoicing in Radnorshire as there was elsewhere, showing that Puritanism had as yet made only a beginning in the county.

## 3. The rise of Nonconformity

It has already been seen what steps government in London in the early days of the Commonwealth took to encourage the spread of Puritanism in Wales; however, even before this unexpected official encouragement, there had been some evidence of native Puritan stirring in Wales. In 1639, for instance, at Llanfaches, near Newport (Gwent) the first Nonconformist chapel in Wales was consecrated, by William Wroth, who from 1611 to 1638 had been the vicar of Llanfaches, until he was turned out for his 'Puritanical leanings'. This independent place of worship may be regarded as the precursor of Congregational chapels.

Back in Radnorshire, of the various groups of Christian dissenters who took advantage of the freer religious climate of the early 1650s, to interpret the Scripture as they saw fit, special mention will be made of the Baptists and the Quakers, because their efforts seem to have been most fruitful in these early years of dissent. However, with the restoration of the monarchy in 1660, came the rigorous imposition of absolute religious uniformity; Parliament passed a series of acts, whose combined effect was to clamp down severely on all expression of religious dissent. The purpose of this so-called Clarendon Code was to destroy Puritanism root and branch; in the dark days that followed Nonconformists had to meet and worship, in secret, in private houses and wait for this storm of official oppression to blow over. In 1688 there was a second revolution, known as glorious, partly because it was bloodless, out of which emerged, among other parliamentary changes, a Toleration Act (1689), which allowed all Christians who were prepared to subscribe to

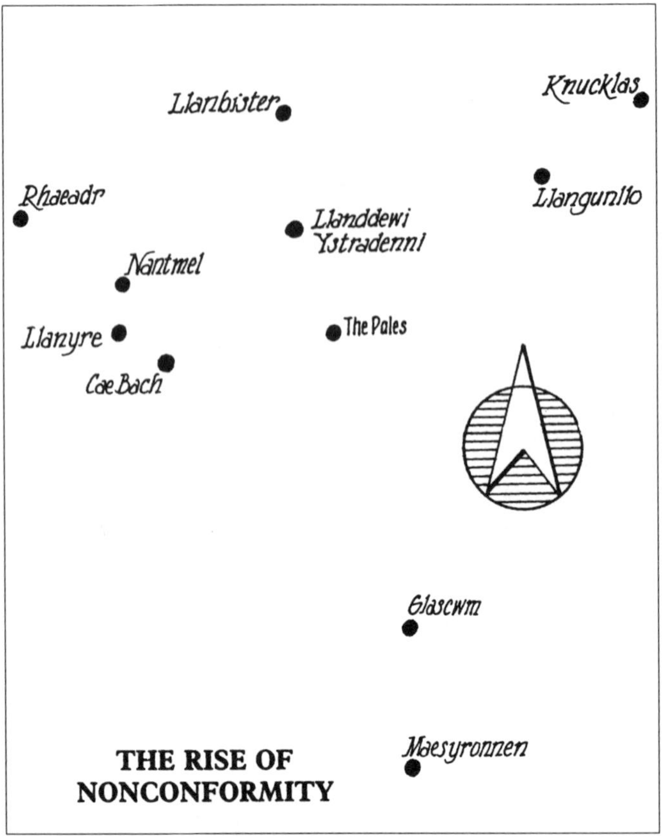

Llanbister

Knucklas

Rhaeadr

Llanddewi
Ystradenni

Llangunllo

Nantmel

Llanyre

The Pales

Cae Bach

Glascwm

**THE RISE OF
NONCONFORMITY**

Maesyronnen

thirty-six of the thirty-nine Articles of religion, in which
the beliefs of the Church of England were enshrined, to
worship freely in their own places of worship. Thereafter,
in direct consequence, in Radnorshire the first
Nonconformist chapels were consecrated.

It seems the Baptist organisers deliberately chose
Radnorshire as their first mission field in Wales; at any

rate it was in Radnorshire that the first substantial Baptist connexion was made. Welshmen were needed for this pioneering work because, although there were already in existence a number of Baptist strong-points in England, no English Baptists spoke Welsh and nothing but Welsh was spoken in Radnorshire at this time. Local preaching campaigns were arranged and, where these were successful, suitable houses were chosen in each locality for future meetings and services. Frequently these safe houses were farms, and certainly by the end of the seventeenth century there were many of these places in the county. In the course of time these Baptist islands tended to develop in two different geographical areas, one in the north, the other in the south. Of outstanding importance in the early years of the Baptist movement in the county were the houses at Llanyre, Knucklas, Llanddewi Ystradenni, Llanbister, Llangunllo, Nantmel, Cefnllys, Llanfihangel Nant Melan, New Radnor and Glascwm.

There were two Welsh Baptists to whom particular credit has to be given for early success, Radnorshire men both, Hugh Evans and Vavasor Powell; their gifts and contributions to the cause were different but complementary. The less famous of the pair was Hugh Evans, though in retrospect his local success in Radnorshire was much greater. Not much is known of his early life, beyond the fact that he had been apprenticed to a clothier in Worcester before moving to Coventry and London. In 1646, during the Civil War, fired with religious enthusiasm, he came into Radnorshire and settled in Llanyre, a village about a mile north-west of where Llandrindod now flourishes. His purpose in coming to Radnorshire was religious, his intention to spread the Baptist cause. To this end, working from his home base in Llanyre, he bore witness to his religious beliefs in various villages in the neighbourhood, including Cefnllys, Nantmel and Llanddewi Ystradenni; other Baptist helpers at that time were John Price (Nantmel) and Henry Gregory (Llanddewi Ystradenni). For ten years, from his arrival in Llanyre in 1646 until his death in 1656 Evans and his fellows laboured hard and well and with considerable success, although his last days were saddened by the realisation that the Quakers, who were active at the same time and in the same part of the county, succeeded in winning over many Baptist adherents.

The other outstanding Baptist leader, Vavasor Powell, was born in 1617, at Knucklas, two miles north-west of Knighton in the Teme valley; educated at Oxford, he first became a schoolmaster, teaching for a while at Clun, before becoming religiously inclined. In 1640 he first fell foul of the law, being arrested for disturbing the peace by preaching! Two years later he was in trouble again, being tried at the Radnorshire Assizes in Presteigne for 'inconformity'; he was however discharged. In 1644, despite his disinclination to conform, he became Vicar of Dartford in Kent, but by 1646, with the Civil War virtually over, he had thrown in his lot with Parliament, being authorized in September of that year to spread Puritanism in Wales. Thereafter Powell achieved much fame as an itinerant preacher in Radnorshire; so speedily did he acquire a reputation as an impressive speaker that in 1650 he was ordered to preach before the House of Commons, as honour which the same year led to his being appointed, after the passage through Parliament of the Act of the Propagation of the Gospel in Wales, one of the experts, empowered to carry out the provisions of the new act in Radnorshire There, in 1655, he joined forces with Hugh Evans, the two great Baptist stalwarts working together at last, though Evans was to die the next year. By this time Vavasor Powell had turned against Cromwell and suffered imprisonment for his pains; as his subsequent career mostly concerned events well away from Radnorshire interested readers will have to make do with the bare information that, with the restoration of the monarchy in 1660, troubles crowded round him thick and fast, resulting in his imprisonment from 1661 to 1667, a further trial in 1668, and more imprisonment in the Fleet Prison in 1669, where he died the following year.

In the improved religious climate after the passing of the Toleration Act of 1689, the Baptists began to plan the building of their own places of worship; which were gradually to take the place of the private houses, which had kept the movement gong in the dark years of persecution. The first such Baptist chapel to be built in Radnorshire was consecrated in 1722 near Pen-y-bont; it was called The Rock.

The early history of the Quaker movement was almost entirely the history of one man, George Fox, a Leicestershire man, born in 1624, who in the early 1640s questioned the validity of the beliefs of the Church of England. He began to act upon his beliefs in 1647, during a time of great civil turmoil, when many long-held opinions were under review; in that year he set out to tour the whole of England and Wales, preaching in the open air, whenever and wherever he could find an audience, over and again denying the need for creeds or sacraments, denouncing all priests of whatever denomination, and asserting that it was essential for every man and woman to have a direct and personal relationship with God.

High up in the remote hills of Radnorshire, east of

Pen-y-bont, there is a Quaker Meeting House, which owes its existence to the personal influence of this remarkable man, who, as early as in 1654, had acquired a few enthusiastic followers in Radnorshire, two of whom, Thomas and Elizabeth Holmes wrote to tell him of successful Quaker meetings they had attended. Three years later, in 1657, Fox came to see for himself; his presence was clearly expected, as a great number of people had foregathered on Pen-y-bont Common, where some sat on horse-back, while others stood around to await the arrival of Fox, who, later, in his Journal, referred to the great gathering, which he had, for three hours, addressed, standing on a chair. He had a Welsh friend with him, who presumably acted as interpreter; he was to pay two further visits to the district in 1663 and 1666. In 1673 a local farmer, who had been greatly moved by what George Fox had said at the first meeting sixteen years before, died, leaving in his will a piece of land, which was to be used as a burial ground for Quakers, whose bodies at death, like those of other non-Anglican Christians, were denied burial in consecrated ground.

Repression grew ever more rigorous during the reign of Charles II, as earnest religious malcontents tried to evade the provisions of the law; all Nonconformists suffered, none more so than the Quakers, some of whom were arrested in 1683, while attending a meeting in their burial ground. They were tried, convicted, fined and many were imprisoned. This was the beginning of Quaker persecution in Radnorshire, but mercifully for the Quaker movement in general a Quaker leader appeared at this time, William Penn, who was to present the Quakers with an alternative to prison and persecution. Penn, the son of an admiral, who had been sent down from Oxford for being a Quaker, had been many times arrested, and several times imprisoned, even in the Tower of London, but when his illustrious father died, William inherited considerable wealth, which enabled him in 1681 to go to America, where he bought a tract of land, which he named, in honour of his father, Pennsylvania. This piece of land, and the settlement of Philadelphia, which he built there, became a safe haven for a great many Quakers from the British Isles, including many from Radnorshire, whose ranks back home thereafter became very thin indeed.

Back in Radnorshire, in 1717, on a piece of land, immediately adjoining the burial ground, the Pales Meeting House was built, where to this day Quakers rejoice to hold their meetings (GR 138641). Today, a little gate separates the burial ground from the forecourt of the thatched meeting house, which is divided into two parts; in the room on the right services take place in surroundings that have changed but little over the years, with some of the furnishings as old as the house. Next door, where, in the nineteenth century a Quaker school flourished, can be seen Quaker books and pamphlets, displayed on a hand bier. This Quaker outpost, meeting-house and burial ground, eleven hundred feet up, with wonderful views across the valley to the Llandegley Rocks, is a living tribute to the Quaker movement and a timely reminder of the courageous men and women, who more than three hundred years ago, dared with clear consciences, to defy authority. G. M. Trevelyan, writing about the achievements of the Quakers at the end of the seventeenth century, said this. 'When the Puritan pot had boiled over and been poured away, this precious sediment was left at the bottom'.

In 1672, ten years after the most repressive acts of the restoration settlement were passed, Charles II by the

Declaration of Indulgence made it permissible for Nonconformists to worship in private houses, provided that they were specially licensed for that purpose; in reality that meant that secret houses which had in the past been used for worship could then become legal, when licensed. No special consecrated places of worship could be contemplated, however, before the Act of Toleration 1689. The Independents (later to become Congregationalists) first took advantage of this relaxation in the law, when in 1692 the first Congregational chapel was built in Rhayader. Four years later a farm was consecrated and rebuilt as a place of worship at Maes-yr-onnen. This chapel still stands, and is still in use as a place of worship; Maes-yr-onnen (GR 177411) can be found half a mile north of the A38, which runs just north of the River Wye near Glasbury in the very south of the county.

Another early Independent chapel, Caebach (GR 059622), which, like Maes-yr-onnen, is still in use today, was built in 1715, about a mile north of where Llandrindod now stands. At that time there were many Independents in the county (especially in the Rhayader area) who previously had had to worship in private houses. In 1715 Caebach was presumably chosen because of its central position, most of the local worshippers coming either from the Garn district, about four miles to the south or from Nantmel (to the north). A survey of the grave-stones in the churchyard will show the long journeys worshippers were prepared to make; in the lane opposite the chapel may still be seen too the stone stable, built to provide accommodation for the travellers' ponies. The original building was substantially altered at the beginning of the nineteenth century, but it has remained largely unchanged for the past hundred and fifty years. In March 1851, when a nation-wide census was taken, the morning attendance at Caebach was thirty-seven, while fifty-two worshipped in the afternoon; had the census been taken in the summer months the attendance would probably have been much larger.

Methodist readers of this chapter on Nonconformity may well be feeling resentful at the lack of reference to their great movement for religious reform. Nevertheless it has to be remembered that the great seventeenth-century pioneers in the field of religious change in Radnorshire were the Baptists, the Quakers and the Independents; it was later – in the eighteenth century – that the yeast began to rise in the Methodist Movement. The spread of Methodism in Wales coincided with the life of Howell Harris, who was born in 1713; by 1740 the movement had gained considerable momentum as the partnership between Harris and Daniel Rowland developed. Dissatisfied as Howell Harris was with the state of the church in Wales, he, like his great English contemporary and friend John Wesley, intended above all to reform his church from the inside; it is perhaps significant that, when Howell Harris died in 1773, his funeral service took place in the parish church at Talgarth. Indeed the break between Methodists in Wales and the parent church was delayed for another thirty-eight years, as it was not until 1811 that an independent Methodist church came into existence in Wales.

The foundations of Nonconformity have already been seen to have been laid in the seventeenth century by brave and zealous Christians, who dared to swim against the tide, but the full consequences of their actions were not fully to be realised until the nineteenth century, when the Methodists, late-starters though they were, began to make startling progress. It is of course no coincidence that the meteoric rise of Methodism in Wales in the first half of the nineteenth century accompanied the sudden and largely unregulated industrialisation of the most heavily populated valleys in south Wales and of the coal-fields in north-east Wales.

In 1801 most Welsh people still regarded themselves as being attached to the established church; by 1830 the Baptists were still the most numerous Nonconformist denomination in Wales, though the Methodists were catching up fast, but in the census returns of 1851 eighty per cent of all Welshmen claimed to be Nonconformists, with the Methodists leading the field; it has to be added, of course, that in those years from 1801 to 1851 the population of the country had doubled.

## 4. Notes and Illustrations

### a. Charles I in Radnorshire

Attention has already been drawn to the brief sojourn of Charles I in the county on his way back home from a rather desperate attempt to rally support in south Wales, after losing the battle of Naseby. Early in August 1645 the King travelled eastwards from Painscastle to New Radnor. In 1870, when the Victorian diarist Kilvert was curate at Clyro, he found evidence of this royal excursion in the folk memories of Radnorshire country people. On March 26th 1870 the diarist, resting for a few minutes in an old house in the hills north of Clyro, asked, in the course of a conversation with an old man, if 'he had ever heard any talk of Charles I ever having been about in this country'. 'Oh yes', he said, 'I have a jug that the King once drunk out of . . . his army was with him and riding two and two in the narrow lanes . . . all the farm people, boys and girls, ran out to see the King pass . . . the King was

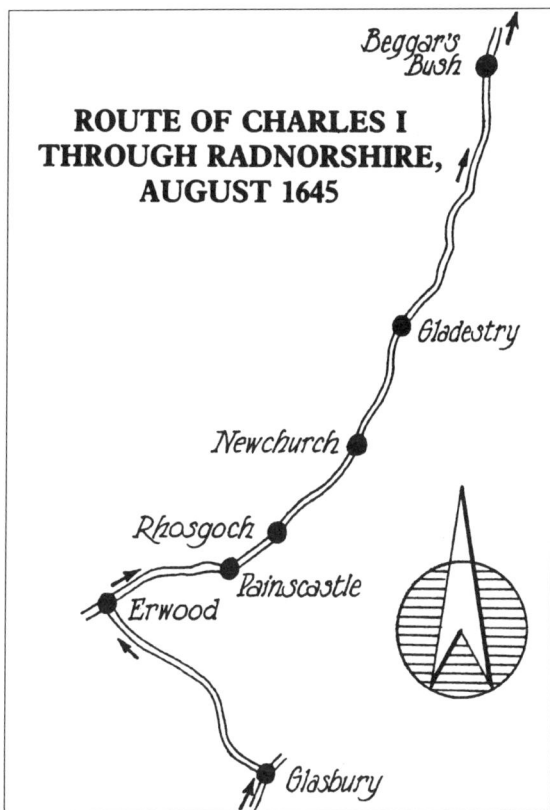

**ROUTE OF CHARLES I THROUGH RADNORSHIRE, AUGUST 1645**

Beggar's Bush

Gladestry

Newchurch

Rhosgoch

Painscastle

Erwood

Glasbury

afoot . . . He stopped opposite the house and asked my ancestress, Mary Bayliss to give him something to drink. She went to the house and fetched him milk and water in this jug, which has been handed down with the tradition in my family . . . I never learnt that the King gave her anything in return for the draught.'

### b. Baptist burial ground at Glascwm

One of the earliest Baptist groups was at Glascwm, where a farmer called John Lewis, in whose house services were held, gave a piece of land to act as a Baptist burial ground; in the event he was the first to be buried there. Kilvert on the 22nd May 1871 walked over the hills from Clyro to visit the Vicar of Glascwm. In the course of a lengthy entry he noted ' . . . Just outside the churchyard the Beavan family (the local squire) has a private burial ground, unconsecrated, where a number of them are buried.' Kilvert was mistaken but was only reporting what he had been told. In fact, the Beavan family had taken over the Baptist burial ground and used it for their own purposes. The little burial ground today is wild and overgrown and quite untended; a recent visit, with a suitable implement for removing moss, revealed the presence of five Beavan table tombs (in an advanced stage of decay) and seven or eight horizontal slabs of early Baptists, one of which, that of John Lewis, was decipherable.

### c. Methodism at Devanna

Devanna (GR 072710) is a farmhouse, a mile east of Abbey Cwm Hir; its name is a corruption of Tŷ Faenor (manor house), the land north of the house being still known as Tyfaenor Park. This splendid old house, a three-storeyed affair, built in the second half of the seventeenth century, changed owners in 1818, when the Griffiths family moved in. They were ardent Methodists in a district where there was no Methodist place of worship; thereupon they started a habit, which continues to this day, of holding services in a room on the ground floor. Here will be seen the well-worn pews which generations of Griffiths have occupied; Devanna is still the focal point of Methodism in this remote and beautiful part of Radnorshire.

### d. Social gatherings in church and churchyard

From the Middle Ages onwards the parish church and the churchyard constituted a community centre; throughout the Middle Ages the north side of the churchyard remained unconsecrated, as did the nave of the church, which in consequence acted as a parish hall. Such being the case, it is hardly surprising that much that went on in the church and churchyard had little obvious connection with the exercise of religion!

Fives were frequently played against the outside walls of churches, especially against the towers, whose buttresses added to the enjoyment of the sport, while dancing on the north side of the churchyard was a regular feature on all special occasions, above all in Radnorshire. In addition every church had a patron saint, whose annual commemoration involved not only a special service in the church but also much secular jollification in the churchyard, which, when the weather was unaccommodating, was transferred to the nave. Many of these secular activities lasted longer in Radnorshire than elsewhere in Wales. Interesting accounts of such celebrations in the churchyard on patronal days survive for three Radnorshire villages, Disserth, Aberedw and Llanbister.

In 1744 a Shropshire lawyer, on holiday in Radnorshire, participated in the celebration of the patronal saint both at Disserth and Aberedw, and, happily for posterity, committed his observations to paper. He described how on his way to Disserth (GR

034583) he fell in with a man, who was leading a horse and cart, which bore a cask of ale for the church celebrations. The little lane that runs down to the white church was crowded with cheerful parishioners, as was the north side of the churchyard, where many were dancing to music provided by a fiddler; in a nearby barn more couples were also dancing, while several games of fives were being played against various walls of the church. The visitor was much impressed by the general happiness of the occasion and found nothing to criticise in the behaviour of the participants. When he reached Aberedw (GR 080474) he was to witness similar sights, games and dancing, and, of course, much eating and drinking. The huge porch of Aberedw church was being used by the musicians; between the two very large yew trees in front of the porch many were dancing.

Llanbister (GR 111734) certainly continued to keep up the annual celebrations of their patron saint until almost a hundred years ago; there on the great day the saint was well remembered by the devout in a special service in the church, which was followed by much secular activity in the large and hilly churchyard, where there was very much eating and drinking as well as dancing, where the slopes allowed. The parishioners had their own special way of remembering St Cynllo; every years, in the middle of July, the churchwardens, who were there, as elsewhere, virtually the wardens of the community centre, nominated certain house-holders to whom the task devolved of making a local delicacy, a large rice pudding, fortified by as many raisins as it could be made to hold. After the service on the patronal day these rice puddings were carried to the church, where they were placed on the walls of the churchyard, and there cut into suitable slices before being speedily devoured!

All good things come to an end! Certainly some of the goings-on got out of hand, as the beer and the cider flowed too freely. Attitudes too were changing, especially with the growth of Nonconformity. In 1840 the Society for the Suppression of Sunday Wakes was formed and by the end of the century the sounds of happy laughter had vanished from the churchyards of Radnorshire, along with the strains of the village fiddlers.

### e. Three nineteenth-century vicars

Price, Rees and Lloyd, spoken together, have the comfortable ring of a prosperous firm of Welsh solicitors. In fact they are the names of three unusual country parsons in Radnorshire in the nineteenth century. If more attention is devoted to John Price than to the other two, it is because he was visited in his hovel in the hills by Kilvert, who could himself almost be regarded as another Radnorshire parson; for, despite his Wiltshire origins, he was a curate at Clyro for some years and later vicar of St Harmon, north of Rhayader, before crossing back over Offa's Dyke to officiate at Bredwardine.

The first of these parsons was the Rev. David Lloyd. The son of a Radnorshire farmer, he served a curacy in Herefordshire before becoming vicar of Llanbister in 1789, the year when the French Revolution broke out. He was to stay in Llanbister for the rest of his life, ministering to the parish for forty-nine years. He is said to have been a man of many interests, which included music, poetry and science; indeed he is credited with having tried for nearly fifty years to make a machine capable of producing perpetual motion! That these interests did nothing to detract from his main task, the care of a very large parish, may be deduced from the fact that in 1826 the Bishop of

St Asaph confirmed no fewer than five hundred and six parishioners in Llanbister church. That same year, 1826, saw the opening of the road from Newtown to Llandrindod, now the A483, and the bishop's carriage, bearing him to the confirmation service, was the first to use the turnpike road. The annual celebrations of Llanbister's patron saint, which took place on the first Sunday after July 17th, had by the nineteenth century deteriorated into drunken revels. Rev. David Lloyd, we are assured, became so concerned at this debauchery that one year in the early 1820s he prayed long and earnestly for divine intervention. So successful did his prayers appear to be that on the appointed Sunday a terrifying thunderstorm broke over the district, dampening all thoughts of excesses, and producing wide-spread flooding! After his death in 1838 a splendid memorial stone was erected in the church; he was, according to this stone, 'purely evangelical in his ministry'. He was certainly a very broad-minded evangelist too, because one day, while he was riding his horse round the parish, he chanced to hear the sound of some hymn-singing proceeding from a farmhouse. He discovered that local Methodists were in the habit of gathering in the farmhouse to hold their services. Thereupon he promised to build them a place of worship; a glance today at the date-stone on the Methodist chapel, which is at the other end of the village from the parish church, will show that the Rev. David Lloyd was as good as his word. The date is 1830.

A brief détour of a mile to the north is here recommended to give the visitor a chance to see the little church at Llanno (GR 097744), which lies to the west of the A483 between the road and the river Ithon. In the 1870s the medieval church was rebuilt but several features of the earlier church were retained, including the octagonal font, a 17th century churchwarden's pew and an exquisitely carved early 16th century screen, to which expert craftsmen later added 25 figures to the loft. Of the many remarkable screens, still to be seen in Wales, few are better than this one of Llananno.

Up a green and narrow cul-de-sac two miles from the B4357, itself a country road west of Knighton, is the remote and isolated hamlet of Cascob, whose thirteenth century church, dedicated to St Michael, stands high up in a huge, raised, circular churchyard. From Bronze Age times onwards men and women have lived on or near this site, the present church being merely the latest in a long succession of buildings. Until the Turnpike Trust in 1767 re-routed part of the London to Aberystwyth road, west of Presteigne, Cascob will have been of some importance. It will certainly have seen then far more people than it ever does today. In 1805 there was a new vicar there, the Rev. William Jenkins Rees, the second of our parsons, who, like his colleague and contemporary in Llanbister, was to spend forty-nine years ministering to the needs of the parish. When he died in 1855, the parishioners erected in the chancel a tablet to his memory; this stone is still there to enlighten passers-by about his outstanding qualities and achievements. He was, above all, a noted Celtic scholar, 'author, antiquary, magistrate, priest and man of letters', the inscription proudly proclaims. He was joint author with Jonathan Williams of a history of Radnorshire, which is still a valuable source book for early events in the history of the county; he also edited the great twelfth century inventory, the *Book of Llandaf*, and played a vital part in preparing the minds of his fellow countrymen for the revival later in the nineteenth century of the national eisteddfod. All in all, the Rev. Jenkins Rees was a very remarkable man and he had, too, the great good fortune to live in what is still one of the most beautiful wooded valleys in eastern Wales.

Llanbedr, the church where the third parson officiated, is a mile west of Painscastle, up a side lane off the B4594 which runs down to the Wye valley below Builth Wells. Kilvert passed that way in 1865 and commented on the ruinous appearance of the church, which he again noted on his second visit seven years later, when he was on his way to see the Rev. John Price in his ramshackle loneliness up in the hills. Whatever the state of the church, John Price was vicar there from 1859 to 1895. The son of a Welsh yeoman farmer, he was ordained in 1834, after leaving Cambridge. He served six curacies before coming to Llanbedr, where there was no vicarage and a very meagre stipend. He stayed a bachelor and acquired the reputation of being a recluse; indeed Kilvert always referred to him as The Solitary. He was to live in various humble and unorthodox places, but when Kilvert tracked him down on Llanbedr Hill in 1872, he was living in appaling squalor. Kilvert thus described the Solitary as he opened the door to him. 'He was a man rather below the middle height, about sixty years of age, his head covered with a luxuriant growth of light brown hair and his face made remarkable by a mild thoughtful melancholy blue eye and red moustache and white beard'. Kilvert went on to tell of the interior of the cottage of which he said 'the foulness and wretchedness of the place is undescribable, almost inconceivable'. Yet, despite these surroundings, John Price had succeeded in devising and getting published a method of shorthand, the efficacy of which he there and then demonstrated to Kilvert.

Around such a character legends were bound to

crystallize. It seems that in an attempt to increase his tiny congregation he invited tramps to come to church and agreed to pay them sixpence a visit. In consequence his congregation grew larger, with the result that John Price found it a financial strain to continue with the sixpenny subsidy. When he told the tramps that he proposed to reduce the sum to four pence, they withdrew to the churchyard to consider the offer. Reluctantly they gave in but, when at a later date, the vicar tried to reduce it to three pence, the vagrants refused to accept the further cut. What effect this had on church attendance is not known. It is known, however, that in an effort to raise the moral standards of this same section of his congregation, he agreed to marry the tramps free of charge. In addition he gave to each couple the not inconsiderable sum of five shillings. Report has it that thereafter some couples managed to get themselves married up to six times by suitably changing their names! This truly remarkable and saintly man lived long enough to see his church reroofed and properly rebuilt. He signed his last death certificate on March 9th 1895, just two weeks before his own death at the ripe age of 85. He is buried in a grave, marked with a white cross near the south door of the church. As late as in 1967 there was still alive in the parish an old couple in their mid-nineties who remembered him. Their comment was 'He was small of stature, a perfect gentleman and kindly disposed'. His memory is surely enshrined in the Hall of fame.

(This chapter originally appeared in the January 1986 number of the *Country Quest*, whose editor authorises its reproduction here.)

*Rhydspence Inn*

Among the surviving inns that supplied the needs of the drovers in the county are the Drovers' Arms in Howey, near Llandrindod, the Forest Inn near Llanfihangel Nant Melan, and the Rhydspence Inn (GR 243473). The first inn on this site, erected in the 14th century, provided for travellers who had forded the Wye nearby, while its 16th century successor, shown in the illustration, supplied the needs of drovers who came with their flocks over the hill from Painscastle.

The surviving cider-press not only confirms the popularity of the drink with drovers, but also indicates the proximity of the inn to Herefordshire. Indeed the national boundary passes through the inn, making it necessary for drinkers in former times, when Wales was 'dry' on Sunday, to move further along the bar into Herefordshire!

*Baptist Burial Ground at Pen-y-bont*

This illustration shows a part of the extensive burial ground, adjoining the Baptist chapel at the Rock, Pen-y-bont (GR 094659); it is to be found up a steep hill, off the A483, just north of Crossgates. The chapel, built in 1721, was the first Baptist chapel to be consecrated in Radnorshire.

*Quaker Burial Ground at the Pales, Llandegley*

This well-kept burial ground is on the hill-side across the valley from the Llandegley Rocks; it dates from 1673, though there were no named graves before the 19th century.

*Independent Chapel and Burial Ground at Maes-yr-Onnen*

This independent chapel in the far south of the county, not far from Glasbury, dates from the late 17th century and is still in use. In the adjoining burial ground there are about thirty graves, the earliest dated 1838.

*Baptist Burial Ground, Glascwm*

A Beavan table tomb can be seen in the background, while the horizontal ledgers in the foreground mark local Baptist graves.

*St Cewydd's Church at Disserth*

*Aberedw Churchyard*

Between the two yew trees dancing used to take place, to which the fiddlers played the accompaniment from inside the immense church porch.

*The Grave of the Rev. John Price*

The churches of the Rev. David Lloyd (Llanbister) and the Rev. William Jenkins Rees (Cascob) have already been illustrated; here is the grave at Llanbedr Painscastle of the third priest, the Rev. John Price (The Solitary), marked by the cross in the foreground.

# IV. The towns of Radnorshire

Today there are four main centres of population in the county, Rhayader in the far north-west, Knighton and Presteigne in the border country, and Llandrindod, the 'new' town in the west. The underpopulated area in the south, which in former times tended to crystallize around Painscastle, is today served, at least in part, by Hay, which, lying just over the river Wye, is not in Radnorshire.

In the Marches, long before Knighton or Presteigne achieved size or significance, the chief centre was New Radnor, whose importance has been described earlier in this book, when its castle figured so prominently in this troubled part of the Marches in the Middle Ages. Even after the castle's day was done, the town that had grown up to supply its needs – and which today is happily by-passed off the busy A44 Kington to Rhayader road – continued to be a place of some substance, being recognised as the county town, when the Act of Union in 1536 officially created the county of Radnorshire. As another part of the 1536 settlement new courts of law were set up for Wales; for dealing with the most serious crimes Wales was divided into circuits, which judges were to visit four times a year. In Radnorshire, Rhayader and New Radnor were chosen to host these courts alternately, but Rhayader had to forfeit her turn when, after a judge was murdered in the town, all future sessions were ordered to be held only in New Radnor, until Queen Elizabeth transferred them to Presteigne. Nevertheless New Radnor retained its status as a borough until 1833. That New Radnor had been overtaken in wealth and importance by Presteigne was made quite clear in the 17th century, when Charles I in 1636 imposed Ship Money; New Radnor had to contribute £6, while more prosperous Presteigne was made to pay £28. Over the centuries, however, there has been very little variation in the size of the population of New Radnor, which in the 17th century numbered about 400, a number which it has never since exceeded, but which has never dropped below 300. After becoming the county town in Elizabeth's reign, Presteigne, as will be seen, went from strength to strength, until the suppression of the 1536 boundaries in 1974 saw the restoration of the ancient regional boundaries of Wales. In this new, modern Powys the chief administrative responsibility went to Llandrindod.

## 1. Rhayader

The original name of Rhayader was Rhaeadr Gwy, the Waterfall on the Wye, a description that is no longer applicable as the waterfall disappeared at the time when the stone bridge was built over the river in the eighteenth century. The earliest inhabitants in the area, as far as is known, were the people of the Bronze Age, who settled in the south at Llanwrthwl, to the east of Rhayader, quite near today's town, and more especially in the north-east, around St Harmon; of these settlements little visual evidence survives.

Christianity came to this part of Radnorshire in the 6th century, when Cynllo, the contemporary of Teilo and Padarn, set up llans thereabouts in Llangunllo, Llanbister, Nantmel and Rhayader. So influential was this missionary that this area later became known as Cynllibiwg, the land of Cynllo, sometimes referred to as Cynllib. Of this first Christian church in Rhayader

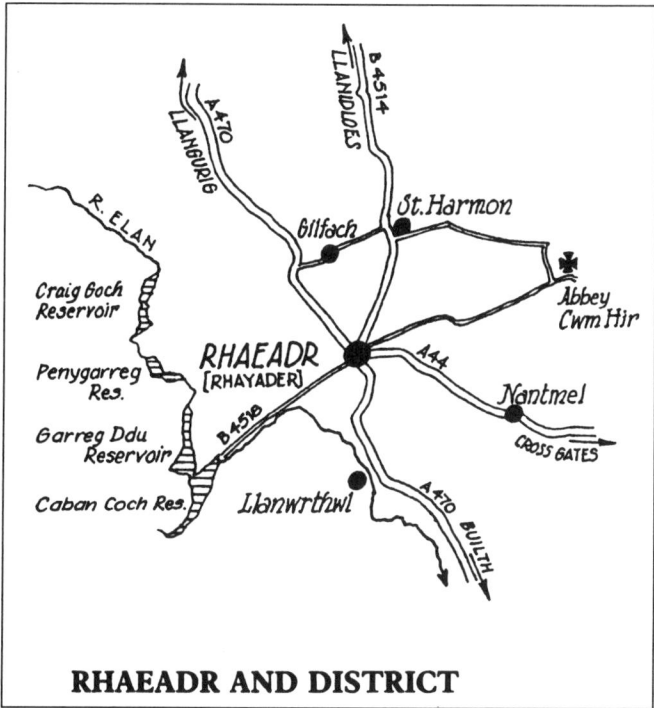

**RHAEADR AND DISTRICT**

nothing at all remains, except the site on which the modern parish church stands; even the dedication has changed, Clement having taken the place of Cynllo. Nearby there was a holy well, dedicated as always to St Mary (Ffynnon Fair), but of this there is now no trace.

Six hundred years later, in the twelfth century, the powerful Rhys ap Gruffudd, later to be known as the Lord Rhys, came north from Dinefwr Castle, near Llandeilo, in Cardiganshire, from where he ruled the large territory, known at that time as Deheubarth. Giraldus Cambrensis, whose contemporary he was (as

153

well as being his nephew), always referred to him as the Prince of South Wales. In 1177, after successfully holding in Cardigan what can reasonably be described as an eisteddfod, to which poets and bards from Gwynedd in the north were invited, the Lord Rhys rode to Rhayader, where later that year he caused a stone castle to be built. Readers of this chapter who have not yet visited Rhayader, are strongly recommended to park their cars in the car park west of North Street, and from there to walk down the lane westwards to a large and flattened green mound, which stands high up on the east bank of the river. Here once stood the Lord Rhys' stone castle, which presumably he built to mark what he hoped would be accepted as the northern boundary of his domain. Seven years later he gave a charter to the Cistercian order, which enabled the monks to build a monastery at Strata Florida, which is only fifteen miles west of Rhayader, as the buzzard flies! (Indeed the great man was buried in the abbey grounds, when he died in 1197.)

A few years later Rhayader castle was burned down in circumstances which have already been described earlier in this book. It was, however, subsequently rebuilt, and before long captured by the Norman overlords in the Marches, the Mortimers, in whose custody it remained until the day in 1231 when Llywelyn ap Iorwerth recaptured and dismantled it.

Geography has played a significant part in determining Rhayader's history; it has already been seen that it owed its castle to its position more or less halfway between the south and the north of Wales. Furthermore it was at Rhayader, which faces the Cambrian Mountains immediately to the west, that a direct route over these mountains became feasible. The clue to Rhayader's geographical position is clearly given by the naming of the four streets that meet at the central clock tower in the middle of the town, North, South, East and West Streets. From the Middle Ages onwards there had been traffic from beyond the Cambrian mountains into Rhayader, much of it being of cattle, which were destined either for the local market or for markets further east in England. Hence over the centuries Rhayader has possessed a very important cattle market on which originally its prosperity was built up.

During the first half of the 17th century life in Rhayader seems to have been little affected by distant events in London, the bitter civil strife of the 1640s sending few shock waves through this part of Radnorshire. The increased freedom of speech, however, which followed the setting-up of the Commonwealth after the execution of Charles I in 1649, allowed many differing opinions to be expressed, which gradually acquired greater volume, especially when the state of the church in Wales was being discussed. Encouraged by the criticism of it by the official commissioners, who toured Wales 1650-3, itinerant preachers went round the county openly giving voice to Puritan doubts, which gradually encouraged ordinary people to start thinking for themselves and even interpreting the Bible as their consciences saw fit. The earliest Puritans in Radnorshire were probably Baptists; it is known that very soon after the monarchy was restored in 1660 and religious censorship reimposed, Baptist missionaries in Radnorshire, where the Baptist movement was at its strongest, looked around them and nominated at appropriate intervals suitable so-called 'safe' houses, where Baptists might meet without interruption. As far as is known, the nearest safe house to Rhayader was at Nantmel, where also early Congregationalists (for such

these early Independent Puritans became) met in a
farmhouse in the parish of Nantmel, named Neuadd-
lwyd. When the Toleration Act of 1689 allowed some
lessening of repressive attitudes towards Christian but
non-Anglican worship, Congregationalists, who had
previously gathered in Nantmel, built a church in
Rhayader in 1692. This first Congregational church in
Radnorshire had as its first minister a very remarkable
man called Thomas Walters, whose ministry there lasted
for sixty years; he died in 1752 and was buried in
Rhayader. It is reported that in 1700 the average
congregation at his church, in Rhayader, numbered four
hundred, which included forty men, of sufficient wealth
and standing in society to qualify for the right to vote.
This vast congregation must have been drawn from great
distances, as was a similar congregation a few years later
at Caebach in Llandrindod. Also in the second half of the
seventeenth century the Quakers were very active in
furthering their cause and in gaining a foothold in
Radnorshire; one example of their success was at
Rhayader, where they were given official permission by
the Quarter Sessions to hold their annual meeting in the
old Market Hall.

Rhayader in the past was much involved in the
movement of men and beasts, but first about men; by the
early years of the eighteenth century the state of even the
main roads in England and Wales was so bad that in 1706
Parliament created the first Turnpike Trust, whereby
commissioners were empowered to erect toll-gates, the
proceeds from which were to be applied to the
improvement of main roads. As the century wore on
attention too was paid to improving the springing of the
coaches, with the result that traffic greatly increased on
such roads as the Great Road from London to

Aberystwyth, which passed through Rhayader, to the great satisfaction of the local inn-keepers, who played Mine Host to travellers.

As to the movement of cattle, the main drover route to pass through Rhayader came from an assembly point in Cwmystwyth, from where the drovers slowly made their way over the Cambrian Mountains, at an estimated speed of twelve miles a day, before breaking their long journey at Rhayader, where the need of the cattle to be reshod as well as the need of the drove masters and their assistants to be housed, brought much life and noise and business to the town. This particular route of the drovers after leaving Rhayader passed through Pen-y-bont, New Radnor and Leominster en route to the English market.

Turnpikes and tollgates, which did much to increase transport in the eighteenth century, became in the 1830s and 40s the object of men's pent-up fury, which culminated in an ugly outbreak of violence. The centre of discontent was south Wales, where acute social misery and general economic discontent were rife. Suffice it to say that public anger boiled over; to the leaders, who dictated the course of events, the most visible reminders of the quarrel with authority was provided by the tollgates, the subsequent attacks on which became known as the Rebecca Riots, a name which touched the Welsh imagination, its memory still alive today, somewhat embellished with the accretions of time! As to the name, in Genesis, chapter 24, verse 60 Abraham chose Rebecca as Isaac's wife. ' . . . they blessed Rebecca and said to her 'LET THY SEED POSSESS THE GATE OF THOSE WHO HATE THEM' ''. The Rebecca Rioters rode the countryside at night, an all-male company, many of them with blackened faces, some of them arrayed in feminine attire, spreading terror among those who looked after the toll-gates. From 1839 to 1843 Rebecca confined her activities to south Wales but in October 1843 she rode into Rhayader, where at that time there were six toll-gates on the six approach roads to the town. First the rioters pushed over two gates on the Llangurig road, an act which led to general rioting in the town. The climax came on November 2nd 1843 when fifty armed rioters marched in three separate parties into the centre of Rhayader, where they joined forces on the St Harmon road; there they destroyed the toll-gate before moving on, in military formation, to the other gates, four of which they destroyed, despite the efforts to stop them of a metropolitan police sergeant, sent from London, assisted by six special constables. Early in 1844 Rebecca again destroyed a gate on the Llangurig road, but this was the rioters' last fling, as the Government, by this time thoroughly alarmed, set up a commission of enquiry, which visited Wales, taking evidence of local grievances in Rhayader in November 1843. Peace thereafter returned to the roads of the town.

There is a curious footnote to the Rebecca Riots in Rhayader. Shortly after the trouble with the toll-gates, local residents were much affronted by a new Fisheries Act, which made illegal the taking of salmon from the Wye. In consequence, from 1850 to just before the first World War, salmon-poaching in the district was widespread because it had been hitherto accepted as a local right to take salmon from the river in summer in order to dry it for winter use. The practice continued, despite the attention given to the poachers' activities by the police. These poachers were always known as Rebecca, who had in consequence a much longer life in Rhayader than elsewhere in Wales!

In 1892 yet another act of Parliament greatly affected

life in and around Rhayader; this was an Enabling Act, which allowed Birmingham Corporation, in its search for an ample water supply, to build a series of reservoirs in the very beautiful Elan Valley, five miles west of the town. This very considerable engineering feat was completed by 1904, and was later supplemented by the construction of a much larger, fourth dam between 1946 and 1952. Today there is an excellent Elan Valley Centre, which has much to commend it, including an audio-visual theatre. The valley is still wild and beautiful, despite the intrusion of man, the bird life in particular being outstanding. The effect of the creation of the Birmingham Waterworks on life in Rhayader was, of course, enormous, bringing many jobs and much money to the town.

Rhayader today is however a holiday town in its own right, attracting anglers, walkers, bird-watchers, pony-trekkers, and indeed all who enjoy unwinding in an unspoilt and still remote area. Rhayader is also fortunate in that in recent years the Radnorshire Wildlife Trust has turned a derelict farm into a Nature Reserve. Gilfach, (GR 965118) lies three miles north of the town, to the east of the Llangurig road. All Nature Reserves are special places, this one at Gilfach is specially special!

*Castle Site at Rhayader*

This flattened green mound above the Wye was where the Lord Rhys built his castle in 1177.

*Gilfach (in 1988)*

The derelict farm as it looked when bought by the Radnorshire Wildlife Trust in 1988.

*Gilfach (after restoration)*

The headquarters of the Nature Reserve as it appears today.

## 2. Knighton

Strangers on their first visit to Knighton might be excused for thinking that it was a busy, but rather shapeless place, built on several levels, with wide streets here, and narrow roads there, without any obvious reasons for such eccentricity. Superficially indeed there seems no pattern, but sometimes history and geography combine to dictate the development of settlements, as indeed was the case with Knighton. The light of understanding may begin to dawn when the Welsh name for the town be remembered, Trefyclawdd, the town of the Dyke; there was no human habitation in Knighton before Offa took up the cudgels on Mercia's behalf, although there had been a Bronze Age settlement not too far away to the west and considerable Iron Age activity in the neighbouring hills. Until nearly the end of the eighth century, however, the Teme had flowed peacefully to the south-east through uninhabited countryside.

In the seventh century the Middle Saxon kingdom of Mercia began to expand westwards, a movement which in the following century initiated a long period of struggle between the Mercians and the Welsh, culminating in 784 in a strong retaliatory Welsh attack, which the men of Mercia had the greatest difficulty in containing. In the next decade, in a lull in this long-drawn out power struggle, Offa put into effect his plan to impose an eastern boundary on the Welsh. However, a continuous, unbroken line of defence would not only have been hard to maintain, it would in addition have prevented Offa from being able to keep contact with the Welsh with whom he needed both to trade and to achieve some sort of understanding. Thus in constructing his dyke, Offa saw to it that at suitable intervals there should

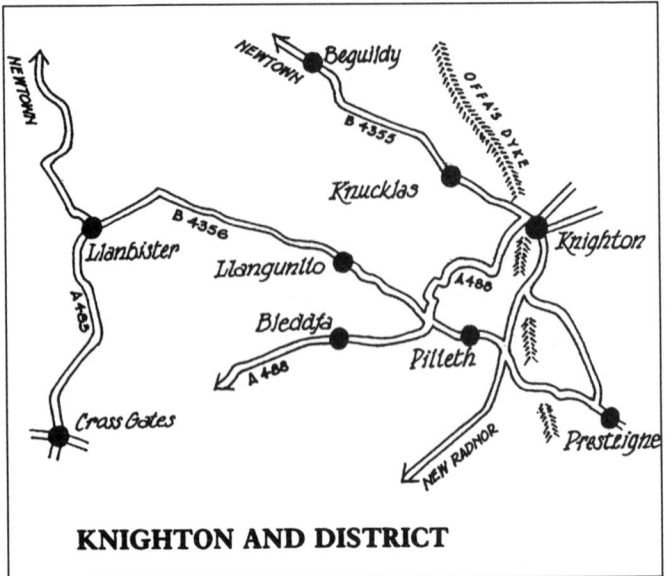

**KNIGHTON AND DISTRICT**

be gaps where contact could be made, where goods could be exchanged and where, with sensible precautions, access might be granted to Welshmen to pass into Mercia and for Mercians to enter Wales. This circumstance gives the necessary clue to the origin of Knighton; the very first settlement there needed as much protection as possible. Hence it was sited in the limited area bounded by the Wilcome Brook and its confluence with the Teme, below the spot where the Dyke came down from the hills to the river. This is then where Knighton began. Piecing together Knighton's early history, it seems that in this Mercian settlement down by the Teme, immediately south-east of Offa's Dyke, a church was built somewhere between 1042 and 1052, a church, which was dedicated to Edward the Confessor, who was King of England from

1042 to early in 1066. The present church stands on this original site. (This same Edward the Confessor owned a castle at Womaston, north-west of Kington, which was itself named after the same monarch.) Further evidence of Christian activity hereabouts in the Middle Ages is provided by the use made of Jackets Well, half a mile west of Knighton; in Bronze Age times this well supplied water to the local community, but by the Middle Ages the church authorities had made it a holy well and for centuries Christian sufferers from rheumatism went there to take advantage of its healing properties.

It is known that in 1052 the Welsh attacked and captured Knighton, the possession of which they managed to keep until the Normans took it back in the early years after the Conquest. They were to consolidate this recapture of the place by erecting a large motte and bailey near the river in about 1100, Bryn-y-Castell – this mound still stands. A few years later the Normans decided to build elsewhere; this time they moved away from the river and went up the hill, where it would be easier, they hoped, to defend themselves. Here, on a site above the Wilcome Brook, they put up another castle to which were later added stone ramparts and other defensive works. This new strong point was put to the test when Llywelyn ap Iorwerth (the Great), having taken by storm New Radnor castle, advanced upon Knighton; in 1213 the castle fell to the great Welsh leader. Henry III, who was much preoccupied with the defence of the Marches, empowered the Mortimer family, whose base was Wigmore Castle in Herefordshire, to see to the recapture of Knighton, which indeed the Mortimers soon succeeded in doing. In 1262 however the Welsh again attacked, this time under the command of the former victor's grandson, Llywelyn ap Gruffudd (the Last), and again captured the castle and town, but before long the Mortimers returned victoriously to Knighton.

The fourteenth century passed without much military activity but the unusual lull ended at the beginning of the fifteenth century, when the mighty hero of Wales, Owain Glyndŵr, challenged the authority of England, wherever he came up against it. As a thrust against Knighton became imminent, Edmund Mortimer brought in four hundred trained soldiers from Ludlow to defend the castle, but all in vain, as Owain Glyndŵr captured and virtually destroyed it in 1402; in a few years Glyndŵr's meteoric career came to a sudden end and so once again Knighton reverted to the Mortimers.

The uncertainty about whether a Welsh prince or a Marcher lord should control the destinies of Knighton, was brought to an end by the Act of Union in 1536, by which the county of Radnorshire was created from which two men were to be elected to parliament in London, one to represent the interests of the country districts, and the other to be selected by the burgesses of the five recognized boroughs, New Radnor, Rhayader, Cefnllys, Knucklas and Knighton. Never again was Knighton to see fighting, either down by the river around Bryn-y-Castell or higher up in the town, around the later castle.

A century later Knighton was but little affected by the turmoil of the Civil War in the 1640s, but inevitably became involved in some of the changes that followed the death of Charles I and the setting-up of the Commonwealth under Oliver Cromwell, when for the first time religious dissent was openly expressed. Three miles up the Teme valley from Knighton is Knucklas, where lived one of the most prominent of early dissenters, Vavasor Powell, who, it is known, debated doctrinal matters with his fellow Baptists in a house in

Knighton in 1658. It is also known that in the second half of the 17th century, after the monarchy was restored in 1660 but before Parliament by the Toleration Act of 1689 allowed dissenters to have their own places of worship, Quakers held their annual meetings in a private house in Knighton. Methodism was a much later Nonconformist development, the actual break with the established church in Wales not coming until 1811, but in 1818 one of the first, if not the very first Methodist chapel in Wales was consecrated in Knighton. Methodists may also be interested to learn that Howell Harries, the acknowledged father of Welsh Methodism, married a Radnorshire girl, Ann Williams.

From the middle of the 17th century Knighton, which had in 1230 acquired a charter to hold a weekly market, had served above all as a market town, where sheep and cattle were bought and sold. In an earlier chapter an account was given of the way Welsh cattle arrived at their eventual markets in England. Several of these drovers' roads passed through Knighton, one coming from Cwmystwyth, via Llangurig, Llanidloes, Llandinam and the Anchor Inn (which was for very many years popular with the drove masters), while another, also from West Wales, choosing a more southerly route, came through Llanbister, and Llangunllo, before leaving the main droves near Pilleth and moving north-east to Knighton. In addition many smaller and less-organized groups of cattle were driven over the hills to Knighton, where they were regrouped, before being driven again in larger droves to their destinations somewhere in England. This cattle trade, which had grown piece-meal in the Middle Ages, continued well into the 19th century, indeed until, with the coming of the railways, an altogether different mode of transport was provided. In 1865 the arrival of the railway in Knighton on its way to Llandrindod and ultimately to Swansea, did much to open up Radnorshire, with a considerable increase of population and prosperity in the Knighton area.

Today some visitors to the town in their haste to move westwards either by road or by rail (should it survive the trauma of being privatised!) may not realise how much they are missing, if they do not explore the quiet beauty of the Teme valley, where there is much to make the thoughtful traveller stand and stare. Bronze Age people have left their memorials in the valley in the shape of round barrows, one of which is well preserved on the west side of the Teme (GR 223770). Further along the B4355 is the village of Beguildy, which in former times was the centre of a prosperous sheep-rearing area (Beguildy in its Welsh form of Bugeildy means 'The Shepherd's House'). St Michael's Church, built on a hill in the middle of the village, has in its large round churchyard many excellent specimens of the stonemason's art. This Teme valley has many other treasures, which it will divulge to those who venture further afield beyond Beguildy.

No account of contemporary Knighton is complete that ignores the importance of the Offa's Dyke Long-distance Footpath, which was officially opened in 1971. Since then many more people than hitherto have come to know Knighton, as they scramble down off the dyke. Responsibility for the upkeep of the dyke rests with the Offa's Dyke Association, a voluntary body, whose headquarters are fittingly in Knighton, their address being Offa's Dyke Association, West Street, Knighton, Powys LD7 1EW.

## Bryn-y-Castell, Knighton

On the wooded hill, illustrated here, above today's playing fields the Normans erected a wooden castle in about 1100, when they recaptured Knighton from the Welsh, who had successfully taken it from the Saxons in 1052.

Before long Bryn-y-Castell was superseded by another wooden Norman castle, built higher up in the 'Top of the Town'. This second castle was later rebuilt in stone.

## St Edward's Church, Knighton

Today's church occupies the original site, where the first church in Knighton was erected sometime between 1042 and 1050. It was dedicated to Edward the Confessor, who was King of England from 1042 to 1066. This church was the centre of the Saxon settlement down by the river Teme, near where Offa's Dyke crossed the river.

*The Old House, Knighton*

Above the Clock Tower in Knighton's busy town centre is this medieval timber-framed house, a part of which dates back to the 15th century.

## 3. Presteigne

Presteigne is much more obviously an old town than are most places of a similar age; to start with, it has not grown very much over the centuries and has therefore not covered its ancient buildings with modern ones in the way that many old towns have done. Indeed but for the ubiquitous presence of the motor-car, which the present-day one-way system in Presteigne can do but little to diminish, the past still dominates, revealing itself, as it does, in a great many old houses. Of modern facilities Presteigne has its fair quota but they do not tend to clash with the old but rather blend with them to impart a sense of the past participating in the present.

In general terms a town's history is often paralleled in the development of its parish church; while this is mostly true of St Andrew's church (the Welsh name for Presteigne is Llanandras) it has to be added that the earliest stones in this church, which are Saxon, can find no corroboration in any surviving buildings near the church. Nevertheless historians believe that traces of Saxon work in the church confirm the meaning of the original Saxon name of Presteigne, which was Presthemede, indicating that priests had lived thereabouts. The picture thus presented is of an early settlement, consisting of a huddle of Saxon dwellings clustered around the church near the river Lugg; this settlement, which had preceded the arrival of the Normans, was seriously damaged in a raid made in 1052 by Gruffudd ap Llywelyn. About a hundred years later the newly-arrived Normans built another settlement in Presteigne, high up above the river in the Warden, where they erected a motte and bailey, of which the mound still survives. The eventual joining together of this Norman

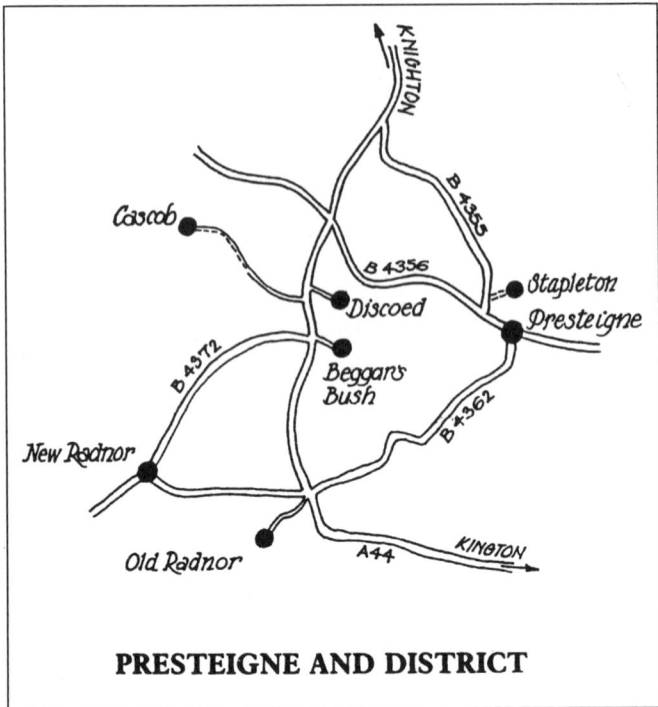

**PRESTEIGNE AND DISTRICT**

settlement around the castle in the Warden with the earlier Saxon one around the parish church gave rise to medieval Presteigne.

About a mile north-east of the town, over the three-arched stone bridge, and therefore in England, is the hamlet of Stapleton, which, it perhaps needs to be said, was a planned town, built by the Normans in the twelfth century; indeed for some years Stapleton threatened to outshine Presteigne in importance, receiving permission to hold a market as early as in 1216, some years before Presteigne was granted a similar privilege. By 1300 the populations of the two towns were about equal. To the curious visitor in the quiet and narrow lanes around Stapleton today all this is hard to believe, as there is now little enough evidence to confirm the recorded facts. Even the stone ruins of the 'castle' refer only to an 18th century building.

Life in Presteigne in the Middle Ages must have been very difficult and dangerous; the stone castle in the Warden, which the Mortimer family built in the second half of the twelfth century, was stormed and captured by Llywelyn ap Iorwerth (the Great), in 1213, but, though he had later to hand it back, he attacked it again in 1231, this time unsuccessfully. His grandson, however, Llywelyn ap Gruffudd did recapture it in 1262, before proceeding to destroy it; it has never been rebuilt. In the following century, the fourteenth bubonic plague, which ravaged the whole country at that time, reached Presteigne, where from 1367 to 1369 it took a heavy toll of life. Thirty years later misfortune again befell the town, when Owain Glyndŵr in 1401 laid waste most of Presteigne; in the middle of this 15th century the Wars of the Roses also involved Presteigne, because their Mortimer overlords were stalwart supporters of the Yorkist cause. On that bleak February day in 1461, when the Mortimers gained the mastery at the decisive battle of Mortimer's Cross, the Yorkist army had marched out that morning from their base in Presteigne.

When the long-drawn out Wars of the Roses at last ended, very many soldiers, deprived by the peace of their livelihood, took to a life of robbery and violence, all too many of them choosing to establish themselves in the hills behind Knighton and Presteigne. Apparently this thoroughly unsatisfactory state of affairs lasted until well into the 1530s, when the President of the Court of the

Council of Wales and the Marches, operating from Ludlow, decided on a vigorous course of action. He was Bishop Roland Lee, who had received his bishopric as reward for marrying Henry VIII and Anne Boleyn; he proceeded to dispense very effective, if rough justice against the malefactors, who were brought before him at his court in Presteigne. This court of Lee's was in session for eight years, and according to contemporary accounts, with five thousand prisoners being executed, life thereafter in the central Marches became a good deal less dangerous for the law abiding.

In the Act of Union 1536, whereby the county of Radnorshire was created, New Radnor and Rhayader were clearly regarded as the two most important places in the new county, because to them were assigned the responsibility of holding twice a year the Great Sessions, where judges on circuit dealt with all the most serious crimes committed, crimes thought too grave for Justices of the Peace to handle in local Quarter Sessions. By the end of the 16th century, however, Presteigne had grown considerably in prosperity, partly through a busy market and partly because of the profitable manufacture of cloth. Indeed one of the local cloth-makers, John Beddoes in 1565 endowed a grammar school in the town, whose comprehensive successor in the late 20th century still bears his honoured name. Bubonic plague alas struck again in 1593, in 1610 and yet again in the 1630s, the combined effects of which was for a while to have an adverse effect on the manufacture of cloth.

The middle of this seventeenth century was also bedevilled by the quarrel between the King and Parliament, and in the civil war that followed Presteigne sided with the King. A few years later Presteigne became the county town, supplanting New Radnor, which at same time had its right to host the Great Sessions transferred to Presteigne, where they were to stay until a change in the law brought the Great Sessions to an end in 1830, but, as the new assizes after that date were also assigned to Presteigne, it can truthfully be said that all serious crimes in the county were dealt with in Presteigne right up to 1970, when under the Courts Act of that year Mr Justice Mars Jones opened the local Assizes for the last time, although of course the Petty Sessions continues to be held in the Shire Hall in Broad Street.

The eighteenth century witnessed a great increase in road traffic, with better-sprung carriages making long journeys more feasible; the upkeep of the main roads was met by the creation of Turnpike Trusts, the tolls accruing from their toll-gates providing the necessary finance. One of these main arteries of communication in the eighteenth century was the London to Aberystwyth road, known as the Great Road, which passed through Presteigne, to the general benefit of the town, seeing that travellers took advantage of the accommodation provided by the many local inns, of which the most popular were the Duke's Arms in Broad Street and the Radnorshire Arms in High Street. The prosperity brought by this increase in coaching unfortunately for Presteigne came to an end in the 1820s, when the road was rerouted through Kington, there-after following in general the line taken by the modern A44. A further local loss came after the passage through Parliament in 1888 of a local government bill, which brought into being county councils, the first of which in Radnorshire met the following year in Llandrindod.

Through all the changes that the centuries have brought to Presteigne, the sieges, the outbreaks of disease, the spread of industry, the dispensing of justice at the Assizes, the busy market and the arrival and departure of the London coaches, St Andrew's church has stood firm at the bottom of Broad Street above the river Lugg, that is the national boundary. At first sight it resembles a small cathedral, and it is certainly architecturally outstanding among the churches of Radnorshire, sited in a large churchyard, many of whose tombstones provide excellent examples of the stonemason's craft. The church registers started in the 1560s, as did the nightly custom of ringing a curfew at eight o'clock, a continuing custom which helps in yet another way to remind the present generation of the impact of the past.

Between the B4355, which comes from Knighton, and the Lugg, just before Presteigne is entered, will be found between the road and the river heartening evidence of the consideration being given to the future as well as respect for the past. Here is Presteigne's Withybeds Nature Park; two acres of wet-land have been leased by the Radnorshire Wildlife Trust, which with local cooperation is attending to the preservation of the flora and fauna to be found there. The willow, which gives the reserve its name, is one of many varieties of trees, under whose branches thrive all manner of water plants, along with the wild life that flourishes on the ground, in the air and, indeed, in the Lugg.

Back in Presteigne, George Borrow a hundred and fifty years ago is known to have stayed at the Radnorshire Arms; the story goes that on arrival he asked the maid if Presteigne was in Wales or in England. The reply he received, which allegedly was 'Neither, Sir, it is in Radnorshire', commands our attention! There may well have been some truth in this naive reply! For, Presteigne is different, it is something of an oasis, that seems far removed from a world that is overdevoted to getting and spending.

*St Andrew's Church, Presteigne*

The earliest settlement here, Saxon, consisted of a church surrounded by a few huts, just west of the river Lugg; on this same site the splendid 14th century parish church now stands.

*The Shire Hall, Presteigne*

The Shire Hall in Broad Street, above the parish church, was built in 1829 on the site of the former prison. Here formerly the Quarter Sessions were held, though today it has to be satisfied with the Petty Sessions and the County Court.

## 4. Llandrindod

Prehistoric people in the Llandrindod area, at Carreg Wiber, Cefnllys and elsewhere, would not have been able to maintain themselves in their settlements but for the presence in their midst of adequate supplies of water, afforded by their wells. It is a curiosity of history that the prosperity of modern Llandrindod had also been made possible by the existence of springs and wells, though these waters, albeit valuable and of proved medicinal value, would hardly have accounted for the survival, let alone the prosperity of Llandrindod, had there not also been a plentiful supply of aqua pura, as chalybeate and sulphur are tastes acquired by very few indeed!

Little is known for certain about these springs of medicinal water at Llandrindod before the eighteenth century, the earliest reliable information seems to refer to the late seventeenth century. In the middle of the following century a new word appeared in the English language, spa, which, up to that time, had been used solely as the name of a small hill-top town, south-east of Liege in Belgium; here, where medicinal springs had been known to exist since the Middle Ages, doctors in the middle of the eighteenth century started to pronounce them health-giving. Before long this small, largely unknown place had become the most fashionable resort in Europe, and, as such, soon became the model for other places, with similar natural endowments, like Bath and Matlock, Harrogate and Malvern, Buxton and Cheltenham, and, of course, Llandrindod. The modern history of Llandrindod then began about two hundred and fifty years ago, when circumstances combined to make it possible for a town to grow up to supply the needs of those with sufficient time and money to seek cures for their dyspepsia and depression.

Many other springs and wells of medicinal water were to be discovered in central Wales, specially favoured in this respect to the west of Llandrindod being Builth Wells, Llangammarch Wells and Llanwrtyd Wells (all three were in Brecknockshire); to the east medicinal springs of more consequence to Llandrindod's future were opened up at that same time at Llandegley, near Pen-y-bont. Situated on the old Great Road, the eighteenth century coaching road from London to Aberystwyth, Llandegley had a coaching inn, which became a favourite stopping-place for travellers, who would break their journeys there, so as to be able to take advantage of the sulphur springs to be found in the immediate vicinity of their inn. Before long enterprising people found ways of attracting travellers to stay at farms near the wells at Llandrindod, until a Mr Grosvenor, a Shrewsbury business man, appeared on the Llandrindod scene. He it was who built the first hotel at Llandrindod, where he catered admirably for the needs of those who came to take the waters by providing other amenities, such as places in his hotel where his guests might like to dance or play billiards and outside where they could fish or play bowls. This Grosvenor Hotel, not surprisingly, flourished, as did other similar establishments, which offered various grades of accommodation and amenities. In 1787, however, the unexpected happened when the Grosvenor, under a new owner, came to a sudden end; it appears that the new proprietor, who was governed by Nonconformist moral attitudes, according to local gossip, suddenly closed his hotel, when he found out that his house was much favoured by guests who were gambling for very high stakes.

The year of destiny for Llandrindod was 1865, when the Railway arrived; with it came more hotels, more shops, more houses, more amenities of every kind. By

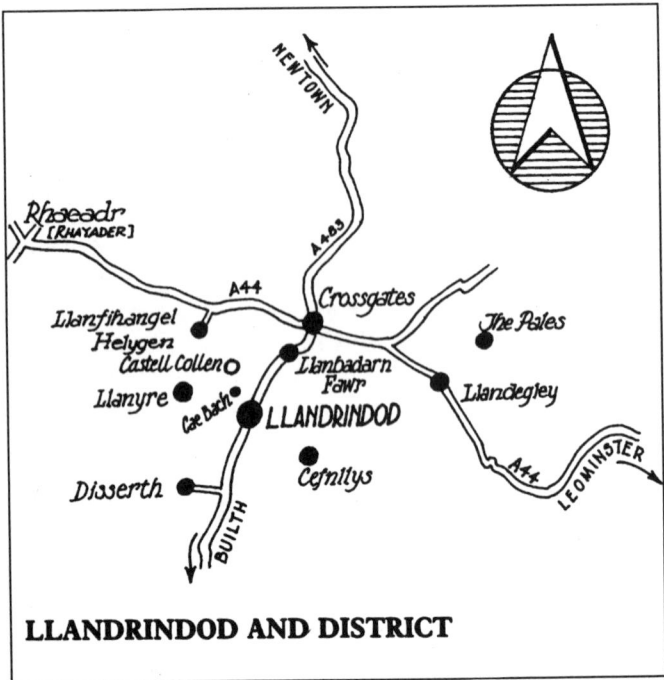

**LLANDRINDOD AND DISTRICT**

1880 Llandrindod had eighty thousand visitors a year. Golf courses were laid out, more bowling greens were prepared, an artificial boating lake were created and most religious denominations was catered for.

It is perhaps advisable here briefly to interrupt this chronological account of the development of Llandrindod in order to let readers know something of the early history of the Christian church hereabouts; the first local church, of which anything is known, can still be seen on a hill above the boating lake up the steep road, which today leads to the golf course. It is about half a mile south-east of the town, is dedicated to the Holy Trinity and was built in the late thirteenth century. There is also another medieval church, a mile and a half to the east of the town at Cefnllys, dedicated to St Michael. Christians in the Llandrindod area in the eighteenth and nineteenth centuries worshipped either at the old church on the hill or at Cefnllys, unless they had Nonconformist leanings, in which case they may well have resorted to Caebach, which, as has already been told, opened its doors to dissenters in 1715.

The railway, it will be recalled, reached Llandrindod in 1865; in the rapid expansion of the spa which followed, among the new buildings to be built was a centrally-situated Anglican church, also dedicated to the Holy Trinity, which was consecrated in 1871. Old habits die hard and, as Anglicans continued to prefer worshipping either at the old Holy Trinity church or at Cefnllys, the local archdeacon decided upon a very strange course of action. In 1893, on his instructions, both these popular old churches had their roofs taken off, in a drastic attempt to change the religious habits of churchgoers. In the very next year, however, public opinion, or it may have been a change of heart on the part of the church authorities, caused both churches to have their roofs put back on again! By the end of the nineteenth century, the spa was more or less complete, with the recent addition of two large hotels, the Pump House in 1886 and the Metropole in 1899. The coming of war in 1914 put the brake on any further development, but 1920 witnessed the consecration in the old parish church above the lake of the first Archbishop of Wales.

At the end of September 1923 the author, then twelve years of age, went to live in Llandrindod, arriving in the late evening in a train, which deposited him and his family on the station platform, in the gathering gloom with a biting east wind to hurry them along. It was a strange beginning to a very happy five-year stay in an unknown world, where everything seemed different but one in which everyone did their best to make the strangers soon feel wanted. At this distance of time, seventy years later, certain memories stand out, like flies in amber. In the season, which began at Whitsun and ended early in September, the many large hotels seemed always to be filled with famous and prosperous guests, whose names, many of whom had handles to them, appeared in long lists once a week in the local paper. In church, on a Sunday morning, at least in the large red-brick Congregational church (now disappeared from view), the offertory plate always seemed about to overflow with ten shilling and pound notes. Well-known people came to conferences in the 1920s, none better-known than Lloyd George, who was still trailing clouds of glory. Down in the Rock Park visitors thronged the spa, imbibing the evil-smelling sulphur water (the chalybeate spring was free to rate-payers, to the dismay of the author, who was expected to take full advantage of the privilege!).

The 'wireless' was still in its infancy and, though most people had sets of sorts, it required a powerful receiver to get good reception. Another happy memory is of being entertained by a prosperous and rather pompous neighbour, who wanted us to be able to share the pleasure of hearing grand opera from Italy, only to be disillusioned by an announcement that ended the recital of gramophone records from Glasgow! Public announcements were still being made by the town-crier, who, armed with a loud hand-bell, rode on a bicycle from point to point, while the motive power for the fire-engine was still being provided by a horse, which was put out to graze in a field at the bottom end of Tremont Road, from where he was fetched, when required, by a perspiring fire-man, who, like the town-crier, was mounted on a bicycle. In the interwar years Llandrindod probably changed but little, still depending very largely on its mineral springs, conferences and bowling tournaments.

The war years from 1939 to 1945 must have been difficult ones for Llandrindod people, but the War Office came to their rescue, when it was decided that an Officer Cadet Training unit should be established in the Metropole Hotel; thereafter for the rest of the war a succession of officer cadets brought welcome economic and social refreshment to the locality. Immediately after the fighting ended, before there could be any proper flow of holiday-makers back to Llandrindod, there was a further piece of good fortune for the place. Officer cadets were followed by teachers in training, when an Emergency Teachers' Training College was established locally. The presence, however, of officer cadets and teachers in training, welcome though they were, could not for long disguise the fact that the old pre-war pattern of taking the waters could not be restored, but, as more and better roads were built and the supply of cars increased, Llandrindod began to take on a new lease of life as a general holiday centre, where a widespread variety of options awaited the holiday makers. Excellent facilities were available for golf and bowls, for angling and rambling; above all Llandrindod became a good centre for motorists, who from Llandrindod could conveniently explore in all directions.

The year 1971 saw the official closing of the Spa in Rock Park, but before long Llandrindod was to strike gold, if that be not too exaggerated a description of the consequences that accompanied the redrawing of the map of local government! In the wholesale reconstruction of local government throughout England and Wales, that arose from the passage of an act of Parliament in 1974, the separate counties of Brecknockshire, Radnorshire and Montgomeryshire were merged together into one very large area, to be known as Powys, of which Llandrindod was made the administrative centre. There was then, of course, much rejigging of existing buildings, and even more construction of purpose-built offices, as the various branches of the new county council were provided for.

In recent years, every September, by which time most of the visitors have gone home, Llandrindod lets its hair down! It is carnival time, when for a week Victorian life is reenacted, with most people seeming to join in the fun, donning Victorian attire. In September 1992 this annual fantasy received wider recognition, when a Victorian morning service from the Holy Trinity church was televised. Some enthusiasts correctly dressed in period costume, each year, even trundle out penny farthing bicycles, which with much skill and courage they manage to manoeuvre in the busy streets of the town.

To historical enthusiasts – and it is to them that this book is primarily directed – Llandrindod's chief attraction today is its proximity to a number of interesting historical sites, three of which, all of outstanding appeal, will now be mentioned, in an attempt to induce readers, as soon as they have finished reading this chapter, to go out and see for themselves.

Within five miles or so all three will be found; an Ordnance Survey map is essential, as are walking shoes. First, north-east of Llandrindod, is the Pales Quaker Meeting House, a mile up a steep and narrow lane, north of Llandegley. The early Quaker burial ground, the Meeting House next to it, and the marvellous setting of the place will make recompense for the effort required to get there. Moving clockwise, the second site is Cefnllys; much has already been written in this book about this wonderful district. If a car is taken, it may be parked at the picnic site at the Shaky Bridge. Whatever the mode of transport chosen, readers are recommended first to walk through the Nature Trail at the Shaky Bridge and on to the Alpine Bridge, where the mound can be spotted nearby on which the Norman motte and bailey was erected. Then climb Cefnllys Hill and walk back the length of it, noting the remains of the Iron Age settlement and the two medieval castles before descending to visit St Michael's church, which is screened by a circle of yew trees. In the field by the Ithon, which separates the church from the Shaky Bridge note the grass-covered humps, which mark the former homes of villagers in this failed medieval town of Cefnllys.

The last place to be visited is the easiest to find, the church at Disserth. Take the A483 southwards out of the town for two miles, then turn right at a cross-roads on to a minor road a mile along which a lane will be seen to the left, which runs down to the river Ithon, where the white church beckons. Something of the popular church patronal festival has already been written, but today the great attraction of the church is its interior, which remains exactly as it was in the seventeenth century. Disserth is one of the very few Radnorshire churches that escaped restoration by the Victorians. The years retreat; box pews, still bearing the names of their occupants, belong to the seventeenth century, as does the triple-decker pulpit. Everything smacks of another age. As readers wander through this time-warp, they may care to muse that, when in 1872 the living fell vacant, the Vicar of Clyro strongly recommended that the next incumbent should through this time-warp, they may care to muse that, when in 1872 the living fell vacant, the Vicar of Clyro strongly recommended that the next incumbent should be his former curate, Francis Kilvert. The bishop alas did not heed the proferred advice – and so there were no accounts of Disserth in the diary.

*The Old Church, Llandrindod*

Holy Trinity church, dating from the 13th-14th centuries, satisfied the spiritual needs of local Christians until superseded by a new church, similarly dedicated, which was built in 1871, by which time a church in a more central position was deemed desirable.

*Castle Hill, Cefnllys*

On this hill, on three sides of which the river Ithon flows, there was first an Iron Age settlement, whose ramparts were later incorporated into an early Norman castle. When that was destroyed, a new and stronger castle was built at the other end of the hill, above the church.

# Index of Radnorshire places

# Further enjoyable reading on History and Heritage

Visit our website for further information:
## www.carreg-gwalch.com

Orders can be placed on our
## On-line Shop

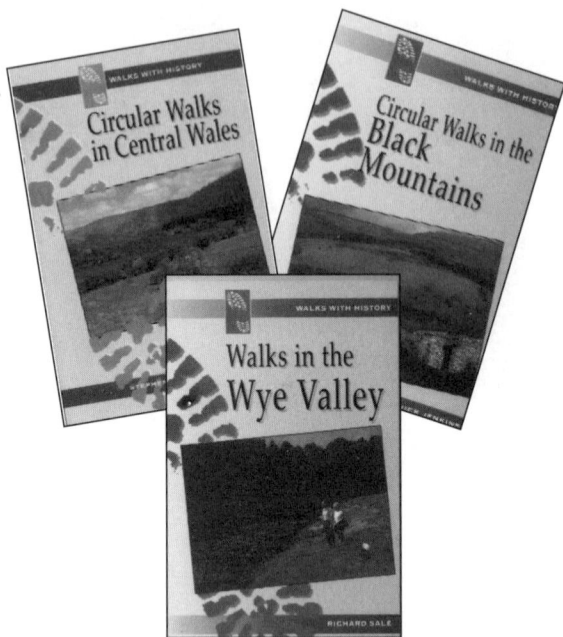

# Further enjoyable reading on Welsh Crafts

# On-line Shop

Our whole catalogue of titles are available on our website

• Walking and Mountaineering
• Regions of Wales / Local Guides
• Maritime Wales
• Welsh Heritage and Culture
• Art and Photography
• Welsh History and Myths
• Children's Books
* BARGAINS *

www.carreg-gwalch.com